# BREACH OF TRUST

## The Ethics Scandal That Challenged the Integrity of the Vermont Judiciary

by James J. Dunn

Onion River Press
191 Bank Street
Burlington, VT 05401

Printed in the United States of America

Publisher's Cataloging-in-Publication data

Names: Dunn, James J., author. | Amestoy, Jeffrey L. (Jeffrey Lee), 1946-, foreword author.
Title: Breach of trust : the ethics scandal that challenged the integrity of the Vermont judiciary / by James J. Dunn ; with a foreword by Jeffrey Amestoy, retired Chief Justice, Vermont Supreme Court.
Description: Includes bibliographical references. | Burlington, VT: Onion River Press, 2018.
Identifiers: ISBN 978-0-997645-8-7-3 | LCCN 2018943305
Subjects: LCSH Judges—Vermont—Discipline. | Judicial ethics—Vermont. | Legal ethics—Vermont. | Vermont. Judiciary department. | Judges—United States. | BISAC LAW / Ethics & Professional Responsibility | LAW / Judicial Power
Classification: LCC KFV520 .D86 2018 | DDC 347—dc23

*Front Cover:* Old Chittenden County Courthouse, Burlington, Vermont.

# BREACH OF TRUST

## The Ethics Scandal That Challenged the
## Integrity of the Vermont Judiciary

### by James J. Dunn

With a Foreword by Jeffrey Amestoy,
Retired Chief Justice, Vermont Supreme Court

ONION
RIVER
PRESS

191 Bank Street
Burlington, Vermont 05401

# ACKNOWLEDGMENTS

This story could not have been written without the extraordinary efforts of reporters from two major newspapers in Vermont, the *Burlington Free Press* and the *Rutland Herald*. Although different reporters from each paper covered the story, special thanks goes to Debbie Bookchin of the *Rutland Herald* and Leslie Brown and James Bressor of the *Burlington Free Press*. Over the course of the four years and more this story unfolded, these reporters followed the story's many twists and turns, attending hearings, speaking with witnesses and lawyers, and reporting in great detail on the hearings and trials before the Judicial Conduct Board, the Rutland District Court, and the many hearings and appeals to the Vermont Supreme Court. Largely through their efforts, this story was voted Vermont's top news story of 1987 by the editors and news directors of newspapers, television and radio stations in Vermont.

This is a work of nonfiction. Most of the events described in the book took place between December 1985 and August 1991. I conducted some interviews of individuals involved in the story, which I try to tell in the 'historical present," using quotations from the newspaper articles appearing in the *Burlington Free Press*, the *Rutland Herald* and the *New York Times*, and from numerous court records and transcript testimony. Thanks to the University of Vermont's Bailey Library, where newspaper articles were stored, indexed and made accessible on microfiche, and to the archivists at the State of Vermont, who preserved the old court records and made the court documents and papers available.

Finally, I want to thank those friends and colleagues who read various drafts of the story. Two former law partners, Neil Mickenberg, and retired Judge Michael Kupersmith, read the early drafts, and their guidance and support helped shape the telling of this story. A special thanks to three individuals who played key roles in the story—former Attorney General and retired Chief Justice of the Vermont Supreme Court Jeffrey Amestoy, former Supreme Court Justice James Morse, and criminal defense attorney William Nelson. Their willingness to read and re-live these events, and to share with me their experiences during those times, helped sharpen the narrative, and hopefully made the story more compelling.

# CONTENTS

# FOREWORD

Interference with a core function of democracy. A cover-up. A concerted effort to discredit the prosecutor's office. A divided public, some urging accountability, others calling the investigation politically motivated, all impatient for answers to the allegations.

Readers of Jim Dunn's meticulous recounting of the judicial misconduct scandal that shook Vermont more than three decades ago will find a storyline that is disturbingly familiar. For those of us who had a part in the drama without knowing how the final act was to end, *Breach of Trust* is a sobering reminder that a just result is not pre-ordained.

In the Trumpian Age the maxim "power corrupts and absolute power corrupts absolutely" is easily grasped. If you were a young lawyer practicing in Vermont in the 1980s, it is difficult to convey one's increasing dismay and disbelief as one witnessed the misuse of judicial power to corruptly advance a private agenda.

Jim Dunn and I, in our respective roles as private attorney and attorney general, were to each confront the consequences of antagonizing Judge Jane Wheel and her friends. I cannot speak for Jim Dunn's reaction to the episode with which he begins this book—the summons to appear before Supreme Court Justice William Hill—but it surely must rank as one of the most startling moments in his life as a lawyer. I had my own "moment" with Justice Hill as readers will learn.

The challenge for any author of narrative history is to convey to the reader (who knows how the story ends), the reality that those in the story did not know what was on the next page. Jim Dunn has met this challenge so successfully that *Breach of Trust* has brought back to me those stomach-churning days when the integrity of Vermont's judiciary was at risk.

Robert Penn Warren observed that readers "are in suspense not only to learn what will happen, but also about what the event will *mean*." One meaning for this reader at least, was contained in the wisdom of one whose consul I sought during those tumultuous events. Responding to my prediction that any step I might take in an investigation of judicial impropriety would adversely affect my legal career, he said: "All you can do is the next right thing."

In *Breach of Trust* readers will learn of unsung persons who did "the next right thing" when the only certainty was that they would suffer the consequences for doing so. If there is a lesson for our times in this Vermont story, it is that public authority can be corruptly exercised only when we wait for others to prevent it.

Jeffrey Amestoy
*Former Vermont Attorney General and retired Chief Justice of the Vermont Supreme Court*

# CAST OF CHARACTERS
*In Alphabetical Order*

Frederic Allen     *Chief Justice of the Vermont Supreme Court*
Jeffrey Amestoy     *Vermont Attorney General*
Lisa Auer     *Justice Hill's Secretary*
Albert Barney     *Chief Justice of the Vermont Supreme Court*
Kevin Bradley     *Chittenden County State's Attorney*
Allen Bruce     *Burlington Attorney*
Brian Burgess     *Deputy Attorney General*
William Collins     *Assistant Judge in Addison County*
Edward Costello     *District Court Judge and Member of Judicial Conduct Board*
David Curtis     *Defender General*
Phillip Cyrkon     *Assistant Attorney General*
Thomas Debvoise     *Dean of Vermont Law School*
Charles Delaney     *Assistant Judge in Chittenden County*
Hilton Dier     *Superior Court Judge*
William Donahue     *Judicial Conduct Board Prosecutor*
John Dooley     *Justice of the Vermont Supreme Court*
Clarence Dubie     *Candidate of Assistant Judge in Chittenden County*
Ron Duell     *Deputy Sheriff in Chittenden County*
John Easton     *Vermont Attorney General*
George Ellison     *District Court Judge*
Fiona Farrell     *Assistant Clerk in Chittenden Superior Court*
Francis Fee     *Clerk in Chittenden Superior Court*
Shireen Fisher     *Member of Judicial Conduct Board*
John Fitzpatrick     *Chittenden County Treasurer*
Victor Fremeau     *Custodian at Chittenden Superior Court*
Alan George     *Counsel for Judicial Conduct Board*
Robert Gaston     *Attorney for Gordon Hunt*
Ernest Gibson     *Justice of the Vermont Supreme Court*
Joan Girard     *Court Reporter in Chittenden Superior Court*

| | |
|---|---|
| Elizabeth Gretkowski | *Assistant Judge in Chittenden County* |
| Paul Hammond | *Probation Officer in Wheel Case* |
| Susan Harritt | *Assistant Attorney General* |
| Thomas Hayes | *Justice of the Vermont Supreme Court* |
| William Hill | *Justice of the Vermont Supreme Court* |
| Phillip Hoff | *Former Vermont Governor and State Senator* |
| Bobby Jo Jackson | *Court Officer* |
| David Jenkins | *Superior Court Judge* |
| Patricia Jensen | *Assistant Judge Washington County* |
| Mathew Katz | *Superior Court Judge* |
| Mary Kehoe | *Burlington Attorney* |
| John Kristensen | *President of the Vermont Bar Association* |
| Madeleine Kunin | *Vermont Governor* |
| Diane Lavallee | *Deputy Clerk in Chittenden Superior Court* |
| Thomas Lerner | *Vermont Court Administrator* |
| Linda Levitt | *District Court Judge* |
| Carl Lisman | *Attorney for Justice Hill* |
| Frank Mahady | *District Court Judge* |
| Maurice Mahoney | *Chittenden County Democratic Party Chairman* |
| Richard Mallary | *Vice-Chairman of the Judicial Conduct Board* |
| Michael Marks | *Attorney for Justice Hill* |
| Stephen Martin | *Superior Court Judge* |
| Francis McCaffrey | *District Court Judge* |
| Earl McLaughlin | *U.S. Marshall* |
| Kevin McLaughlin | *Chittenden County Deputy Sheriff* |
| John Meaker | *Superior Court Judge* |
| Michelle Millham | *Receptionist at Chittenden Superior Court* |
| Randall Moran | *Investigator for Attorney General's Office* |
| James Morse | *Superior Court Judge* |
| William Nelson | *Public Defender Attorney for Gordon Hunt* |
| Jerome Niedermeier | *Federal Magistrate* |
| Harvey Otterman | *Member of Judicial Conduct Board* |

| | |
|---|---|
| Allen Overton | *President of the Chittenden County Bar Association* |
| Roz Payne | *Candidate for Assistant Judge* |
| Fred Parker | *Member of Judicial Conduct Board* |
| Joseph Patrissi | *Commissioner of Department of Corrections* |
| Dennis Pearson | *Attorney for Local Newspapers* |
| Louis Peck | *Justice of the Vermont Supreme Court* |
| Dean Pineles | *Superior Court Judge* |
| David Putter | *Montpelier Attorney* |
| Thomas P. Salmon | *Chair of Judicial Conduct Board* |
| Gregory Sanford | *State Archivist* |
| Kevin Scully | *Burlington Police Chief* |
| William Sessions | *Middlebury Attorney* |
| Kim Sherman | *Deputy Clerk at Chittenden Superior Court* |
| Esther Sorrell | *Chittenden County State Senator* |
| Lewis Springer | *District Court Judge* |
| David Suntag | *Assistant Attorney General* |
| Lee Suskin | *Court Administrator's Office Employee* |
| Percival Shangraw | *Justice of the Vermont Supreme Court* |
| Edward Smith | *U.S. Postal Inspector Handwriting Expert* |
| Terry Trono | *Washington County State's Attorney* |
| Ben Truman | *Chittenden County Democratic Party Chairman* |
| Wynn Underwood | *Justice of the Vermont Supreme Court* |
| James Welch | *Publisher of the Burlington Free Press* |
| Jane Wheel | *Assistant Judge in Chittenden County* |
| Sadie White | *Representative from Chittenden County* |
| David Wilson | *Montpelier Attorney* |
| Leonard Wing | *Attorney for Jane Wheel* |
| Peter Welch | *President Pro Tem of the Vermont Senate* |
| Kinvin Wroth | *Professor at Vermont Law School* |

# PREFACE

The status and importance of judges in our system of government has given the position a special place in our society. Judges are the final arbiters of our disputes, with the final say on the law of the land. Most judges lead active political, professional, and social lives, and have a wide array of friends and professional relationships before they are appointed or elected to the bench. Judicial codes of ethics demand that judges avoid even the appearances of impropriety or conflict, which significantly limits a judge's freedom to associate freely with former friends and colleagues. In discussing some of the ethical challenges facing judges, Connecticut Judge Barry Schaller noted that many judges have great difficulty leaving behind the life they had before assuming the bench, and as a result, they tend to push the envelope of permissible activity even after they have taken the bench: "Their former contacts make it easy to stay connected and enable them to be presented with opportunities that test the ethical limits of judicial involvement in politics."[1]

Since our country's earliest years, the challenge in finding a method to choose our judges has been to find a balance between political accountability and judicial independence—the need for a system to hold judges politically and publicly accountable for their actions, while allowing for the judicial independence necessary to follow the rule of law. Judges were initially appointed by governors, but by the early 1800s corruption and partisanship led more states to start electing judges. In *The Peoples' Court: Pursuing Judicial Independence in America*, Jed Shugerman noted that various judicial selection methods have arisen over the years in an attempt to preserve what he describes as the common theme throughout our history:

> Judges should be separate from politics, that judges should
> be doing something other than voting with public opin-
> ion or voting because of partisanship—that core idea
> of judicial independence animates the story all the way
> through.[2]

1   Schaller, *Ethical Aspects of Political Dilemmas Faced by Appointed Judges*, Yale Law & Policy Review (Jan. 2012)

2   Shugerman, *The People's Courts: Pursuing Judicial Independence in America* (Harvard 2012)

Judges must be seen as objective, impartial, and without bias in matters that come before them. In order to monitor and control the honesty and impartiality of judges, states have adopted codes of judicial ethics, consisting of the standards and norms that bear on judges and cover such matters as independence, impartiality, and avoiding the appearances of impropriety. State judicial commissions or boards are empowered to bring charges alleging violations of the ethics code, to conduct evidentiary trial-like hearings, and to recommend discipline of judges.

While the vast majority of judges in this country are outstanding, ethical jurists, there are a surprising number who stray off the ethical path. In 2015, for example, 115 judges in the country were charged publicly with ethics code violations. Of those, 9 judges were removed from the bench and 21 resigned in lieu of discipline. Of the remaining, 15 judges were suspended and 62 were publicly censured or reprimanded.[3] In addition, an undetermined number of jurists were privately censured or warned.

The potential conflicts for judges differ somewhat between states where they are appointed and those where judges face election, but all judges are held to the strictest ethical rules of any profession. Schaller pointed out the myriad conflicts that arise for appointed judges, who usually must undergo periodic legislative retention hearings, and made this observation about their ethical obligations:

> Serious self-discipline is still very much necessary in order to ensure compliance with all of the requirements of the Model Code. In exercising such restraint, judges are bound to place some restrictions on their personal and professional activities. They must accept the fact that their chosen profession, which is so vital to society, demands their whole-hearted and complete efforts to make their judicial roles their highest priority, regardless of the necessary personal sacrifices that this might require.[4]

From its very earliest days, Vermont adopted a bifurcated system for selecting its judges. Judges for the supreme, superior, and district courts are appointed by the governor. In addition, two citizens, usually non-lawyers, are elected as "assistant" judges in each of the state's 14 counties. Assistant judges serve four-year terms and sit in the superior courts

---

3   National Center for State Courts' Center for Judicial Ethics Report 2015
4   Schaller, Id.

alongside the appointed judges, making a panel of three judges to hear most cases. Vermont's judiciary had remained mostly free from taint of corruption or partisanship over most of its 200-year history. But a murder in Barre in 1982 would find its way to the Chittenden Superior Court in Burlington, and it would serve as the catalyst that would bring together forces and personalities that led to an ethics scandal that would rock the Vermont judiciary to its very core.

In early January, 1987, after an exhaustive and very public investigation, the state Judicial Conduct Board charged three highly respected Vermont Supreme Court justices, all male, with 24 violations of the code of judicial conduct. All of the allegations of misconduct centered around the justices' close personal relationship with a female assistant judge in Chittenden Superior Court, who herself was charged with six ethics code violations. The story told here traces Assistant Judge Jane Wheel's election in 1974 and her rise to power at the superior court in Burlington. It chronicles how Judge Wheel set out to increase the power and influence of assistant judges in the judicial system, and how she carefully cultivated close personal and social relationships with two superior court judges who would later be appointed to the Supreme Court. In late 1985, when Judge Wheel found herself being investigated for allegedly misusing public funds, she didn't hesitate to reach out to her friends on the Supreme Court, and they were only too ready to help.

The story follows the Wheel investigation as it grew into a formal inquest and eventually led to the state charging Judge Wheel with three criminal felonies, making her the first Vermont judge ever to be charged with a felony. The story chronicles the truly extraordinary steps the justices took to intervene in the judicial process to protect Wheel during the investigation. These actions showed an appalling lack of ethical concern or obligation, and led to the unprecedented ethical charges against the justices.

The narrative then breaks into parallel tracks, with one track following Wheel's criminal case as prosecutors from the attorney general's office and Wheel's attorneys prepared to do battle in an epic, four week criminal trial that leads to a final jury verdict. Witnesses, including current and former Supreme Court justices, judges, lawyers, and court personnel, described the actions Wheel had taken and the arrogance she had shown at the courthouse. Chief Justice Allen himself testified as to how the publicity and allegations had adversely impacted the internal workings of the Vermont Supreme Court. On a parallel track, the story follows the three-week ethics trial of the Supreme Court justices, in which the evidence exposed the extent to which the justices went in an effort to protect Wheel. There is the extraordinary testimony under oath of Judge Wheel and Justice William Hill denying they were ever "sexually intimate" with one another despite substantial evidence to the contrary. The ethics trial concluded with the Vermont Supreme Court's final decision on whether the justices should be disciplined for their actions.

This is a story about the Vermont judiciary's dark journey through the greatest scandal in its history. It is a story about arrogance and abuse of power, coupled with allegations of romantic affairs and cover-ups. It is a true story, based on events that actually happened, and all of the characters who appear in the story are real. Friends and colleagues who read the many drafts, and who offered valuable comments and suggestions, all agreed that it is a story that needs to be told, and not forgotten. It is an interesting story in its own right, with a cast of almost a hundred Vermont justices, judges, politicians, lawyers and court personnel. It also serves as a reminder of how fragile our system of justice is, and how, even in the bucolic hills of the Green Mountains, vigilance is needed to preserve the integrity and impartiality of our judges and our judicial system.

# INTRODUCTION

Although the story told here first broke publicly in December 1985, I had my own unfortunate encounter with Assistant Judge Jane Wheel four years earlier. After six years working as a legal aid attorney, I had started a private practice in 1981 together with two of my colleagues in Burlington, Vermont. We had opened our law office in a small building a few doors down from the old Chittenden County courthouse in Burlington. It had served as the county courthouse for a hundred years until around 1970, and thereafter it had been leased to local non-profit organizations. Vermont Legal Aid had leased the old courthouse and moved its offices there shortly before I arrived in the winter of 1976. It was a beautiful building, built with redstone from local quarries. My legal aid office had 20 foot ceilings, with beautiful woodwork and decorative glass transoms over the doors. Our law library was in the massive court room on the second floor, and was used by all the lawyers in town. In 1972 the building was placed on the National Register of Historic Places. In short, it was no ordinary building, and I had a special affinity for it.

We had been gone seven months when, on a bitter cold February night in 1982, the old courthouse burned to the ground—or, more accurately, the roof and entire inside structure of the building burned to the ground. The massive, beautiful outer stone walls and bell tower remained intact, still proud, but now just an empty shell. The Burlington Civic Trust, a non-profit organization working to preserve historic structures, produced an engineering report supporting the feasibility of saving the existing stone walls and constructing a new interior. The two elected assistant judges in Chittenden County, Jane Wheel and John Donahue, had authority over the use of the property, and they announced their intention to raze the building and to build a parking lot to accommodate the new courthouse.

On June 11, 1982 we filed a lawsuit on behalf of the Burlington Civic Trust, specifically naming the county's two assistant judges as defendants.[5] The city joined us as a party in the case to insure compliance with its historic preservation ordinances.[6] Administrative Judge Edward

---

5   I want to acknowledge Attorney Jeffrey Meller, who co-counselled the Burlington Civic Trust case with me.

6   John Franco, a Burlington assistant city attorney, represented the city's interests.

Costello transferred the case out of Chittenden Superior Court, where both Wheel and Donahue sat, and assigned it to Superior Court Judge Theodore Mandeville, who was sitting in Rutland County. We asked the court to issue a temporary restraining order (TRO) prohibiting the judges from demolishing the courthouse until the legal issues raised in the lawsuit were resolved. In order to issue a TRO, a judge must first find that the party asking for the order has a reasonable probability of prevailing on the merits of the case. If so, then the Court must find that irreparable harm would occur if the TRO was not issued. Both criteria must be present. After hearing from us *ex parte* (without the defendants present), Judge Mandeville made the necessary findings, and on June 11, 1982 issued a temporary restraining order prohibiting Defendants "...from demolishing or otherwise destroying the historic Courthouse..." The restraining order was in effect until June 17, when defendants would be given an opportunity to respond to the lawsuit.

A few days after filing the case, William O'Brien, a well-known local attorney and democratic politician, entered his appearance on behalf of Wheel and Donahue. O'Brien filed a motion to have the temporary restraining order dissolved, arguing that, among other things, the judges were immune from suit, and that the county was not subject to the City's historic zoning laws. On June 17, 1982, Judge Mandeville conducted a hearing on whether the temporary restraining order would be continued. O'Brien introduced evidence from a demolition contractor stating that the work stoppage had resulted in costs to the county of $4,992, and further, it would continue to cost the County $800 each day that work on demolition was stopped. He argued that if the court was not going to dissolve the restraining order, it must require the Trust to post a bond to protect the county against possible financial loss. Court procedures did allow for a bond in appropriate cases.

After considering all the arguments and issues, Judge Mandeville ordered the restraining order to continue for an additional ten days. However, in consideration of the alleged costs the county was incurring due to the delay, the judge ordered the Civic Trust to post a bond in the amount of $20,000 by 2:00 pm on Saturday, June 19th. Otherwise, the restraining order would expire and the judges would be free to take the building down. After prevailing on all the legal arguments and winning an extension of the restraining order, the Civic Trust suddenly faced an insurmountable task—raise $20,000 in 48 hours. The Civic Trust certainly didn't have that kind of money, and there was no time to try to raise it. We were pretty much out of options.

As Saturday morning dawned, we decided to mount one last effort to save the courthouse. We called Judge Mandeville at his home in Rutland and made a last minute request for a hearing to ask him to reconsider the issue of the bond. We pointed out to him that, as a legal matter, there was precedent supporting our argument that the requirement of a bond should be waived in this type of case. A few years earlier, the Vermont Supreme Court had seemed to acknowledge that where government or its agents are defendants, the right to waive security is based on the policy that any party adversely affected by government action should have a right regardless of his/her financial situation to seek judicial review of that action.[7]

To our enormous surprise, Judge Mandeville granted our request, and even though it was a Saturday, he offered to either come to the court in Middlebury, which is half-way between Burlington and Rutland, or conduct the hearing by phone. I notified O'Brien, and we agreed to meet at O'Brien's law office for a telephone conference hearing with Judge Mandeville at 10:30 that morning. O'Brien maintained a law office in his stately brick home across from City Hall in downtown Winooski. The Saturday afternoon hearing began with O'Brien on the telephone in his law office, which was just off the living room. I was on an extension line out in the living room. We made our arguments that, as a non-profit organization doing work preserving historic buildings, the Civic Trust should not be required to post a bond.

O'Brien was livid that the Court was still even considering the matter, and argued emotionally against a waiver, reiterating to the Court that it was costing the county hundreds of dollars every day the demolition was delayed. After hearing all arguments, Judge Mandevillle rejected our request to waive the bond. We had arrived at the final moment, and we had lost. The restraining order was set to expire at 2:00 that afternoon.

Normally, individual decisions that are made by a judge in the course of a trial cannot be appealed until the case is fully concluded and a final judgment is entered. However, court rules do allow in certain instances for what are called "interlocutory" appeals, or appeals on certain interim orders or rulings of a lower court before a final judgment is entered in a case. Either party can ask the judge for permission to appeal from an interlocutory order or ruling of the court. If the lower court denies a request, the party may ask the Vermont Supreme Court for permission. You must have

7  *Committee to Save the Bishop House v. Medical Center of Vermont,* 400 A.2d 1015 (1979)

permission—there is no right to an interlocutory appeal. As a last desperate move, we asked Judge Mandeville for permission to take an "interlocutory" appeal to the Vermont Supreme Court on the narrow question of whether the Civic Trust should be required to obtain a security bond in this case in order to maintain the restraining order in place.

The phone line went silent for what seemed like a very long time as Judge Mandeville pondered the fate of the old courthouse. When he did speak, he agreed that the Civic Trust's request for a waiver of the bond had raised a substantial question of law about which there was a difference of opinion. Based on this finding, the judge granted the Civic Trust permission to appeal to the Vermont Supreme Court the narrow question of whether a bond should be required in this case. Judge Mandeville then acknowledged that, without the protection of the restraining order during the appeal, the old courthouse would be immediately razed, rendering moot the entire litigation. The judge found that resolution of the bond issue would therefore likely determine the outcome of the entire litigation, the other important finding in considering an interlocutory appeal. Judge Mandeville ordered that the restraining order be continued during the appeal and until the Vermont Supreme Court answered the following question:

> Must Plaintiffs, who are individual citizen/taxpayers, and a non-profit, public interest organization, post a security bond for injunctive relief to preserve the status quo when they bring suit against government officials for a declaratory ruling of the legal duties of those officials?

O'Brien was beside himself, and stormed out of his house without a word to us. If there was any doubt as to whether he fully understood Judge Mandeville's order, it was dispelled the next day in a newspaper article appearing in the *Burlington Free Press*. The article, with the headline "Legal Wrangling Ricochets Off Courthouse Walls," recapped the history the case had taken to that point, and quoted Attorney O'Brien as accusing Judge Mandeville of an:

> ...'abuse of discretion' in allowing the Civic Trust to appeal to the high bench. He [O'Brien] said he was puzzled by the Judge's first requiring the bond, then refusing to extend the deadline for posting and now allowing an appeal of the requirement.

The days following the hearing were quiet. We drafted an order consistent with Judge Mandeville's decision and forwarded it to O'Brien and the Court for review and the judge's signature. We had won! The old courthouse lived to see another day. The interlocutory appeal to the Supreme Court would take months, and our clients would have the time to build community support to save the old courthouse. On Wednesday, June 23, members of the Burlington Civic Trust noticed activity at the old courthouse site that appeared to be preparation for demolition. We called O'Brien, who claimed to have no knowledge of those activities. More demolition preparation work seemed to be continuing on Thursday and Friday that week. Several more calls to O'Brien's office went unanswered.

Early on Saturday morning, June 26, a telephone call from one of our clients woke me with news that the old courthouse was about to be demolished. I hurried to the site and found the demolition about to begin. Judge Mandeville had verbally issued the restraining order on the phone a few days earlier, but the written order signed by the judge had not yet been returned to us. A Burlington police officer, advised of the situation, told us he would order the demolition to stop if a judge confirmed the existence of the restraining order. We went over to Nectar's on Main Street, a local pub later made famous as the place where the band Phish would get its start, and called Judge Mandeville from a phone booth in the lobby as the officer stood by. Awakened from his own sleep, Judge Mandeville listened as I described the situation, and after a few moments of silence, he informed me that he was not going to get involved over the telephone talking with a police officer. He simply said, "If they [the Assistant Judges] take the building down, they take it down at their peril." I hung up, turned to my clients, and said: "Looks like it's coming down." And it did. The old courthouse was reduced to rubble by late that afternoon.

We may have had some initial hesitation in taking on the courthouse case to begin with and suing the two judges, but there was never any doubt as to what our next move would be. How could this have happened? Are we not governed by laws, and in dealing with lawyers and judges in particular, is it not reasonable to assume that, despite disagreements, the rule of law will be followed? Especially by judges? There was never anything normal about this case. Not only did we sue two judges, but now the judges had violated a court order, and we needed to pursue a contempt of court action against them. What would be the punishment? The building was gone. We could not have imagined ourselves in this position. But there was no hesitation.

On June 29, 1982, with the rubble of the old courthouse still being cleared away, we filed a motion before Judge Mandeville to have Assistant

Judges Jane Wheel and John Donahue held in contempt of court for violating his order. Vermont procedure provided that a motion to have a person held in contempt of court should be filed in the court from which the order issued. Who better to know whether a court order had been violated than the judge who issued the order. Contempt proceedings are based on disrespect for the authority and dignity of the court, and have two purposes: to punish non-compliance with a court order, and to compensate an injured litigant for the harm done by the violation. Vermont law is consistent with the widely-accepted view that courts have inherent power to punish affronts to their dignity and authority.

O'Brien knew he was running out of time. He also knew that he could not allow his clients to end up at a contempt hearing in front of Judge Mandeville, as he knew full well what his clients had done. While the parties were waiting for the Rutland court to schedule a hearing on the contempt motion, O'Brien filed a Petition for Extraordinary Relief with the Vermont Supreme Court. He asked the Supreme Court to take control of the Civic Trust case, and to dismiss the interlocutory appeal that Judge Mandeville had authorized and all related proceedings, including the contempt motion. Petitions for Extraordinary Relief are very rarely filed, and even more rarely granted. They are intended to be used only when the lower courts cannot provide any adequate relief. In this case the assistant judges clearly had a remedy at law in front of Judge Mandeville, with a right to appeal to the Supreme Court if they were dissatisfied with his decision. In other words, there was absolutely no legal basis to support O'Brien's request that the Supreme Court intervene in this case.

We had heard the widely-known rumors that Wheel's friendship with Supreme Court Justice William Hill was more than collegial. And although we had the law on our side, we had already seen, as we watched the old courthouse be demolished, that the rule of law does not always prevail. O'Brien's filing of this petition at the Supreme Court was a last, desperate effort to save Wheel and Donahue from having to face Judge Mandeville and explain why they violated his order. Finally, on July 28th we received notice that Judge Mandeville had scheduled a hearing on our contempt motion for August 6, 1982 at 10:00 am. We were finally going to get our day in court. And we did, just not in the court we thought.

It was a telephone call late in the afternoon of August 3, three days before the scheduled contempt hearing, that let us know we were in serious trouble. The clerk of the Vermont Supreme Court called to inform us that Supreme Court Justice William Hill had just issued an order in the Civic Trust case. It was addressed to each of the four members of the Civic Trust who were the named Plaintiffs in the case. The clerk read the Order to us:

> You and each of you are hereby ordered to appear before the Vermont Supreme Court at its hearing room at 111 State Street in Montpelier, Vermont at 10:00 am on August 6 to show cause why the petition for extraordinary relief filed by the plaintiffs herein should not be granted.

And that was not all. The order concluded with the following:

> A hearing on contempt scheduled for 10:00 am on Friday, August 6, in Rutland against the defendants in the matter of Burlington Civic Trust, *et.al,* v. County of Chittenden, Vermont, Jane Wheel and John Donahue, Assistant Judges, of and for said county, and any other causes now pending, are stayed until further order of this Court.

The Order was signed by only one of the five Supreme Court Justices— Justice William Hill.

Whatever naivety we may have continued to harbor quickly drained away as we struggled to grasp what had just happened. On three days' notice, and without any basis in law whatsoever, one justice of the Vermont Supreme Court had ripped the contempt hearing from its proper venue in Rutland, seized control of the case, and ordered four Vermont citizens to appear at the Vermont Supreme Court in Montpelier to answer why the entire case should not be dismissed. It was beginning to look like there might, in fact, be some truth to the rumors about Justice Hill and Judge Wheel.

The end came quickly, and while I cannot say it was painless, it was not, at that point, unexpected. As I approached the podium in the ornate chambers of the Supreme Court, with the portraits of past justices staring down upon us, I decided to go right to the point. "Why are we here?" I asked the Court. As I began to review the procedures normally followed in a contempt proceeding, I was immediately interrupted by Justice Hill, who proceeded to scold me for bringing a contempt action against a judge, and to administer a verbal bashing the likes of which I had never experienced in the eight years I had been practicing law, nor in the more than thirty years since.

It didn't take me long to realize that it had been over before we had ever gotten there. The facts were not going to matter. Nothing that I said was going to matter. When I had had enough, I closed my file with more force than necessary, muttered something to the effect that "we all know what is going on here," and stepped away from the podium. Shortly thereafter, the Court issued the final entry order in the case. It contained all of six words: "Motion to dismiss granted. Appeal dismissed." Judge Wheel got her parking lot. We went back to our law practice, a lot less idealistic about the rule of law, and about the world we lived in.

We, of course, could not have known that what happened to us was, indeed, a foreshadowing of things to come. Three years later, in the fall of 1985, I received a call from lawyers for the Judicial Conduct Board. Justice Hill was under investigation for some alleged misconduct regarding his relationship with Judge Wheel, and the lawyers wanted to talk about Hill's conduct and demeanor in questioning me in the Civic Trust case. I had not filed any complaints about how I had been treated, and was surprised to be getting called about it. It turned out that things were finally catching up to Judge Wheel and Justice Hill, and they were about to pay an enormous price for their breach of trust.

# PART ONE

*An Inquest Into Improprieties*

# A. STATE v. HUNT

Late in the afternoon on April 19, 1982, Peter Sophos was found shot to death in his first floor apartment in Barre, Vermont, a working class community known for the Italian stone workers who immigrated there in the late 1800s to work with granite from the nearby quarries. The police arrived at the crime scene around 4:30 in the afternoon and began interviewing people in an effort to determine what had happened. Gordon Hunt, a 19-year-old man living with his father in the second floor apartment directly above the victim, told the police he did not see or hear anything unusual, although from the conversation it was apparent that Hunt had been home that afternoon.

As the police began searching the second floor hallway for evidence, they noticed a broken padlock on the attic door. An officer climbed the stairs to the attic, and Hunt followed him up, telling the officer the attic was "private property" and that he "shouldn't go up there." It was dark in the attic, and the officer retreated to get a flashlight. He returned with another officer, and as they climbed the attic stairs, Hunt again attempted to follow them up. The officers ordered him to remain downstairs.

In the attic the officers discovered a rifle hidden behind a cabinet. One of them stayed with it while the other one went to summon the crime lab team and to obtain the landlord's written permission to search the attic. Meanwhile, Hunt had returned to his apartment, opened a window and was preparing to jump to a roof five feet below, when an officer entered the apartment and asked where he was going. Hunt responded he was going to the store. The officer asked him if he would "stick around" for a little while, and he agreed. A short time later the police asked Hunt if he would go down to the station to answer some "routine questions," and he agreed to do so.

At the police station Hunt was interrogated by three officers, one of whom asked him how he could have been in his apartment at the time of the murder, not sleeping or watching television, and not have heard a gunshot. Hunt asked to be left alone with this officer and, before the officer said another word, Hunt confessed to the killing. In a subsequent taped statement, he told the officers that he shot Sophos because he wanted to see what it was like to kill someone.

The state charged Hunt with first degree murder, and because of the enormous amount of local publicity it garnered, a request by Hunt's attorney for a change in venue was granted. The case was moved from the court in Barre to the Chittenden Superior Court in Burlington, where it was assigned to Judge James Morse, the presiding judge, who would hear the case along with the two assistant judges for Chittenden County, Jane Wheel and Charles Delaney.

The role of assistant judges in Vermont's judicial system is carved into the state's history. The position was actually enshrined in the first constitution of the newly-formed independent republic in 1777, some 12 years before Vermont became the first state to join the newly-formed union. The founders of the new republic had an enormous distrust of lawyers, many of whom were supporting England in its fight with the colonies. Lawyers had also supported New York in a fight with local settlers over the legality of the title to land grants settlers had received from New Hampshire, angering farmers and local land owners.

The new constitution called for two citizens to be elected from each county to sit on either side of the lawyer-trained judges, who were appointed by the governor. They became generally known as "side" judges, and as Vermont Law School Professor Kinvin Wroth wrote, the idea "was to have another layer between judge and jury to provide popular input in decisions," and to keep an eye on the lawyer-judges. Vermont was not unique in creating assistant, or lay judges, but in most states they sit on a limited number of lesser judicial matters, such as traffic tickets and small claims actions. Vermont was, and remains, the only state in which non-lawyer judges sit on the state's highest trial court, giving them a significant, if not ill-defined, role in the administration of justice.

Hunt had claimed insanity and diminished mental capacity as a defense to the murder charge. As the case slowly made its way toward trial, Hunt's attorneys and the state reached a plea agreement, which called for Hunt to plead guilty in exchange for a minimum sentence of no more than ten years, with a maximum sentence to be determined by the Court. The parties submitted the proposed agreement to the court for approval. Judge Morse was inclined to accept the proposed agreement. He was concerned if the case went to trial whether the state could prove premeditation, and whether Hunt was sane at the time of the killing. He was also concerned about rulings he had made earlier on the admissibility of the rifle and other evidence police found before a warrant was issued. If his rulings were reversed on appeal, Morse felt it could deprive the state of evidence needed for a conviction. Morse announced his willingness to accept the plea agreement. However, Wheel and Delaney, the two side judges, rejected it, expressing their opinion that the minimum ten-year sentence was too lenient for the crime committed.

Judge Morse had been appointed a superior judge in 1981 by Governor Richard Snelling, and assigned to the courthouse in Burlington. It did not take him long to understand the power and influence Wheel had carefully nurtured during her tenure at the Chittenden courthouse. Although his initial contacts with her were friendly, Morse was warned early on from his colleagues on the bench, including Judges Hilton Dier and David Jenkins, to "watch out" for Wheel. They told him how she would use her "friendly" conversations to garner favors from judges, and attempt to draw them into supporting her in the many intrigues and personality clashes she had going at the courthouse.

Like most everyone in the legal community, Morse had heard the widespread rumors of Wheel's "unusually" close relationship with Supreme Court Justice William Hill, which had begun years ago when Hill was a superior court judge in Burlington. Morse also observed the close relationship Wheel had nurtured with Judge Thomas Hayes, who was also assigned to the Chittenden courthouse. Morse understood that Wheel "could be trouble" and adopted a strategy of keeping her at arms' length, and steering clear of any social interactions with her. Wheel quickly sensed that Morse would not become a confidant, and turned on him, making up things that he supposedly said about her, and trying to turn courthouse staff against him. Morse refused to get sucked into her game, and their relationship was strained

At the time the Hunt plea agreement was presented to the court in August 1983, it was not at all clear that assistant judges had the authority to participate in evaluating and ruling on plea agreements in criminal cases. Morse decided not to challenge the authority of assistant judges to participate in plea agreement decisions, and since that meant a majority of the judges hearing the case had refused to accept the agreement, the court rejected it and Hunt was ordered to stand trial. In a most unusual move, both the prosecutor and Hunt's attorney joined in a motion asking Morse for permission to file an appeal to the Supreme Court for a ruling on the narrow question of whether assistant judges had the authority to reject a plea bargain agreement. Permission from the judge (or the Supreme Court) is needed in order to appeal an interim decision before a case is finally decided. Morse wisely determined that it made sense to get this issue determined by the Supreme Court before going forward with the Hunt trial. He granted the motion, and the case headed to the Supreme

Court to determine whether assistant judges had the authority to participate in plea bargain decisions.

# B. ASSISTANT JUDGE JANE WHEEL

Beverly Jane Wheel was born in Burlington's north end in 1932, the
youngest of five children in a working class family. Jane, as she liked to
be called, attended catholic schools and later taught physical education at
Cathedral High School. She was active in local Democratic Party politics,
where her work was mostly in the trenches, stuffing envelopes, distribut-
ing posters and literature, and generally helping out in city elections. She
was a generally upbeat, confident, strongly-opinionated woman, but had
rarely been in the limelight.

Her long years of faithful volunteer work paid off when she was
awarded with the Democratic Party's nomination for assistant judge in
1974 at the age of 42. The party's nomination pretty much assured Wheel
victory in the general election, as Burlington was controlled by democrats, and Burlington's population dominated the other small towns in the
county. Wheel easily won election to a four-year term in 1974, and was
reelected with no serious opposition in 1978, and again in 1982.

Assistant judges had historically played a very quiet, unassuming role
in the state's judicial system. They sat alongside the presiding judges in
certain limited types of cases, and were empowered to hear evidence and
find facts. Beyond that, their power and authority had been limited by
court decisions and legislative actions. After Wheel was elected an assistant judge in Chittenden County in 1974, she gradually set out to change
that, actively pursuing an agenda designed to increase the power and
authority of assistant judges, and at the same time, consolidating her own
power and importance at the Burlington courthouse.

In the early 1980s Wheel led an effort to form the Association of
Assistant Judges, and was elected its first president. She would go on to
use that organization to both lobby the legislature on behalf of assistant
judges, and to intervene as a party in some cases to represent the interests of
assistant judges in pending litigation. One of the Association's first political
efforts occurred about a year before the Hunt murder case. For years assistant judges had been participating in cases in which by law they were not
legally permitted to. And for years the Supreme Court had held that a case
in which an assistant judge had improperly participated would be presumed
harmless error unless the challenger could prove that the assistant judge, by

his or her presence, had affirmatively changed the results of the case.

That all changed in a 1983 case in which the Supreme Court abandoned its "harmless error" rule, and put the validity of hundreds of cases in which assistant judges had improperly participated at the trial level into question.[8] The public reaction was quick. The local media ran a story claiming that up to 25% of the court judgments in the state could be reversed. Legislation was proposed that would further limit the role of assistant judges in the state's judicial process. As president of the Assistant Judges Association, Wheel worked hard lobbying legislators on the importance of assistant judges, and argued forcefully against any further limitations. Her position as president allowed her to speak on behalf of not only herself, but for all twenty-eight assistant judges in Vermont's fourteen counties.

As the legislative session was coming to an end, the legislature was considering a bill that would have allowed side judges to participate in fact-finding in all criminal and civil cases, but prohibit them from participating in "mixed questions of fact and law." The proposed changes would also have prohibited assistant judges from participating in plea bargaining agreements or sentencing in criminal cases. Wheel was able to successfully orchestrate a vote that defeated the legislation. She left the statehouse after the vote believing victory was hers. What she did not know was that after the vote there was further discussion between some legislators and some of the other assistant judges who had stayed around. Out of those discussions a compromise was reached, and the legislation was brought back up and passed.

The next day Wheel resigned as president of the assistant judges' organization, publicly declaring that she was "deeply hurt and humiliated" over the passage of the legislation. Washington County Assistant Judge Patricia Jensen, who had helped Wheel with the lobbying effort, reported that Wheel had called her the night of the vote and was very upset that some assistant judges had decided to support the bill: "She said she would never set foot in another assistant judges meeting", Jensen said, "She said we had wrecked four months of hard work. I knew better than to talk to her then."

When Jane Wheel was first elected as an assistant judge, William Hill was the presiding judge in Chittenden Superior Court, where Wheel would be sitting. By all accounts, Judge Hill and Assistant Judge Wheel became very close friends. They frequently socialized together at lunches

---

8   *Soucy v. Soucy Motors, Inc.*, 471 A.2d 224 (1983)

or after work, occasionally with other Court personnel, but often just the two of them. Rumors that there was far more to Hill and Wheel's relationship than collegiality were rampant among judges, courthouse staff and much of the local bar. The county sheriff's office was located directly behind the courthouse, and the deputy sheriffs would often notice lights on the third floor of the courthouse late into the evenings, with only Hill's and Wheel's vehicles' in the parking lot. The joke among the deputies was "Yup, Hill and Wheel were working on cases late again."

A year after Wheel's election, Governor Thomas Salmon appointed Hill to the Vermont Supreme Court. Although this meant he would move his chambers to Montpelier, Justice Hill became the Supreme Court liaison to the Chittenden Superior Court. In that capacity he found reasons to visit the Burlington courthouse often, and maintained his close relationship with Wheel long after his elevation to the high court. It is not clear when Hill started to actively intervene to protect Wheel from various problems and troubles she found herself in. We know that as far back as 1982 Hill unilaterally intervened in the old courthouse case described earlier to protect Wheel from facing a contempt hearing, and then orchestrating the dismissal of the contempt case against her.

A year earlier, another judge discipline case also had Hill and Wheel footprints all over it. In 1981 the Judicial Conduct Board had conducted a hearing and had recommended to the Supreme Court that a district court judge, George Fienberg, be publicly reprimanded for inappropriate conduct during court hearings. By the time the Board's recommendations reached the Supreme Court, however, Fienberg had retired from the bench. Without any written opinion or explanation, the Supreme Court voted 4 to 1 to dismiss the misconduct charges against Fienberg because he had retired. Justice Billings strongly disagreed with the Court's majority and wrote a dissenting opinion in which he more than hinted that something nefarious was going on, "I cannot subscribe to the majority view which sweeps these violations under the rug," he wrote, "particularly when the majority fails to articulate any reason or basis therefor. I can only conclude that influences not of record have governed the majority decision." [9]

Billing's reference to "influences not of record" was both mysterious and remarkable. It was like a dangling hook, and Hill took the bait. After reading Billing's dissent, Hill wrote a concurring opinion that opened by declaring that, "It seems fitting that my reasons for this decision be placed upon the record." Hill then went on to address Billings:

> The dissent speaks righteously of 'influences not of record' as reason for our decision today. Such vague innuendo does nothing constructive to resolve the problem at hand, especially since Mr. Justice Billings refuses to divulge what strange conspiratorial forces he perceives lurking in the corners of our decision. [10]

What "influences not of record" were Billings referring to? And why did Hill feel it was "fitting" for him to respond to Billings, and then allude to "...strange conspiratorial forces lurking in the corners of our decision." What was going on here? A clue may be found further along in Hill's concurring opinion. Hill had attempted to justify his decision to not discipline a retired judge by arguing that former judges could still be disciplined as lawyers by the Professional Conduct Board. This, in turn, prompted this retort from Justice Billings, "If this were the case, then assistant judges, who do not need to be attorneys in Vermont, could entirely avoid the disciplinary authority of this Court by resigning from office." Did Hill lead the majority of the Supreme Court in *Fienberg* to an outcome the result of which allowed assistant judges to resign from the bench and avoid disciplinary action? By that time most everyone in the judicial system knew of the rumors of an intimate relationship between Hill and Wheel. It was also well known that Hill was not hesitant to take on other members of the Court when it came to protecting Wheel. How far back did all this go was anyone's guess.

With Hill's appointment to the Supreme Court in 1976, Governor Salmon appointed Thomas Hayes to take Hill's place on the superior court bench. Tom Hayes had been elected lieutenant governor in 1968, where he served one term, and made national headlines when he ordered flags lowered to half-staff after the killing of four students at Kent State University. Governor Deane Davis later returned from out-of-state and countermanded Hayes's directive. Hayes served as a superior court judge for ten years, before he too would be appointed to the high court. Hayes spent most of his time as a superior court judge assigned to the Burlington courthouse, where he too would come to work closely with Wheel. They became close friends, and Wheel would eventually ensnare Hayes in her tentacles in ways he would surely later regret.

---

10   Id.

Wheel's power and arrogance dominated the Chittenden courthouse, where she intimidated court personnel and asserted her own personal beliefs from the bench. Her narrow view in child custody cases was just one example of how she wielded power. The law provided that a custody determination between parents in a divorce proceeding was to be made based on the best interests of the child. Wheel made known her view that it was always in the best interests of the child to be with its mother. She developed a reputation in divorce cases for opposing joint custody in virtually all instances, even when both parents had agreed to all the terms and arrangements of their divorce.

Wheel's hard line on joint custody infuriated members of the local bar. It also angered many of the county's citizens caught up in custody disputes despite having reached agreement on how custody would be shared. One couple was so irate over how they were treated by Wheel that they organized a citizen's group to try to oust her from the bench. Ironically, Wheel's adamant refusal to consider joint custody led directly to some legislative reforms that created a legal presumption that joint custody was in the best interests of the child.

In May 1984, with Justice Hill voting with the majority, the Supreme Court declared in the Hunt murder case appeal that it was within the power of assistant judges to participate in plea agreements in criminal cases. The Court reasoned that it was a factual and largely discretionary question whether or not to accept plea agreements, and that assistant judges had such discretionary authority. It was a significant victory for Wheel, and for assistant judges, but it was not without controversy. Justice Louis Peck issued a strong dissenting opinion, arguing that judicial discretion meant legal discretion, which required the understanding and application of legal standards, principles of law and of adjudicated decisions. He argued that it envisioned the exercise of this discretion by a law-trained judge, and that by participating in this decision and overruling the presiding judge, the assistant judges had exceeded their power.

Shortly after the decision was announced, and with the Hunt case now returning to the Chittenden court for trial, Hunt's lawyer, Robert Gaston, moved to disqualify Wheel from sitting on the case. Gaston had taken the depositions of Attorney General John Easton and Deputy Attorney General Charles Bristow. Based on their testimony in the depositions, Gaston argued that Wheel had inappropriately approached Easton for support in the Hunt case while it was pending at the Supreme Court, and that she should therefore be disqualified from sitting on the Hunt trial.

The state agreed that Morse should decide the disqualification motion based on Easton's and Bristow's testimony in their depositions, which were submitted into evidence.

Morse learned from the depositions that sometime in the fall of 1983, Wheel, who at the time was both a sitting judge on the Hunt case and the president of the Assistant Judges Association, called Attorney General Easton to arrange for a meeting to seek his support for assistant judges. At a meeting a week later, at which only Easton and Wheel were present, Wheel asked Easton to file an amicus brief at the Supreme Court supporting the assistant judges' position that they should have a right to participate in plea bargain decisions. Easton responded by saying that he did not want to participate with the Association because he did not want to "appear to undermine the role of the prosecutor." Easton said Wheel continued at the meeting to attempt to persuade him to support the assistant judges, "She described the size of their organization of Assistant Judges and how all of the Assistant Judges felt very strongly about this principle and all these people could be very helpful to me, and that she herself would like to help me in my political end."

A short time later, Easton got a call from Ray Keyser, a lawyer representing the Assistant Judges Association. Easton testified that Keyser mentioned that "his clients exercise a fair amount of political influence in their particular…counties." Easton told Keyser he would "give a fresh look at the situation," and requested a copy of the Association's brief to review. After consulting with his deputy, Charles Bristow, Easton decided not to file an amicus brief on behalf of the assistant judges. Bristow testified that after he conveyed that message to Wheel, she telephoned him and said:

> …something to the effect that the Assistant Judges'
> Association felt strongly about this issue and that it would
> be clear as to those who were supporters of their position
> and as to those who were not, and that if John Easton
> didn't join there might be possible political ramifications
> for him.

Importantly, Bristow also testified that in a conversation he later had with Chief Justice Barney, the Chief Justice told him "…that Wheel had also contacted him about the case and that his response was that it was totally inappropriate for her to do so and he refused to discuss the case with her."

The day after the Supreme Court heard oral arguments on the authority of assistant judges, Bristow, on behalf of the Attorney General Easton, sent a surprising letter to the Chief Justice reversing Easton's earlier position. The letter stated that:

> ...the Attorney General wishes to convey its availability as an *amicus curiae* on behalf of the assistant judges. While the Office recognizes that the Court was provided with briefs on both sides of the issue, the Office of the Attorney General, nevertheless, wishes to make itself available as a resource charged with the defense of the Vermont Constitution and its officers. In that capacity, should the Court seek further briefing on behalf the assistant judges, the Office would accept such an invitation.

Bristow later received a short replay from the Chief Justice "to the effect that the Attorney General's office is free to do whatever it wants." Easton never did file anything in the case. It is unclear what brought Easton to this change of mind. He was running for governor, so he certainly had motivation to keep Wheel, and assistant judges, as friends. In any event, Hunt's attorney, Robert Gaston, argued that Wheel's contacts with Easton and Barney, and her efforts to affect the outcome of the Hunt appeal, constituted an obstruction of justice. He asked Morse to disqualify Wheel from participating in the Hunt trial.

Morse was faced with a difficult decision. The Supreme Court had just affirmed the right of assistant judges to participate in plea bargaining decisions. On the other hand, he agreed that the evidence before him clearly demonstrated that Wheel's actions during the appeal amounted to an attempt to obstruct justice, and that she should not sit on the case. Morse was unaware of any precedent in which a presiding judge had disqualified an assistant judge from sitting on a case, and it was unclear to him if he even had the authority to do so. If he disqualified Wheel, there was every reason to believe she would again appeal to her friends on the Supreme Court, and his order could very likely be reversed, setting a dangerous precedent.

The court clerk, Frank Fee, suggested that Morse consider transferring the Hunt case to another county, where different judges would sit on the case, and thereby avoid the controversy. Morse suspected the suggestion came from Hill. He gave some thought to the suggestion, but was reluctant to transfer the case. The case had already been pending a long time, he was familiar with it, and transferring it to another county would likely delay the trial even further. Importantly for Morse, neither Hunt nor the

State had requested a change in venue, so for Morse to do so without such a request would be in violation of established procedures, and possibly violate Hunt's rights.

On December 27, 1984, Morse issued a sixteen page decision which he began by pointing out that "the single most important ingredient which gives the judiciary its legitimate place as a separate and independent branch of government is impartiality."[11] Morse used a federal first circuit court of appeals case to set out the standard to be used for determining impartiality,

> The proper test…is whether the charge of lack of impartiality is grounded on facts that would create a reasonable doubt concerning the judge's impartiality, not in the mind of the judge, or even necessarily in the mind of the litigant filing the motion…but rather in the mind of the reasonable person.[12]

The state had defended Wheel by citing one particular Canon in the Code of Judicial Ethics, arguing that her conduct did not amount to a "personal bias or prejudice concerning a party."[13] Morse wasn't buying it, pointing out that "The State…misses the point: 'personal bias or prejudice' for or against a party is not the only reason requiring disqualification on the ground of impartiality." Judge Morse proceeded to review the ethics requirements and concluded that, based on the evidence, "there is no doubt that violations of Canons 1, 2 and 3 are established. A judge who employs threats of political influence to persuade a public official to take a particular action violates these standards."

Morse noted that it did not matter whether Wheel's behavior actually influenced the result of the Hunt appeal. "There is the possibility that it did and at least there is the appearance of impropriety, because the conduct was directed toward influencing the result of the appeal." Morse then asked a rhetorical question. "Is it fair to Defendant, or the State, for Judge Wheel to make further rulings in this litigation?" His answer:

> I think not. Simply put, what happened here was political rather than judicial. While a judge may in confined

---

11   Judge James Morse, Opinion and Order, *State v. Hunt,* Chittenden Superior Court Docket No. 81-83CnCr (December 27, 1984).
12   United States v. Cowden, 525 F.2d 257 (1st ca. 1975)
13   Vermont Code of Judicial Ethics Canon 3C (1)(a)

and circumspect ways act in a political sense from time to time, he or she must maintain scrupulous neutrality about issues in a case in which he or she sits. Once a judge allows political action to contaminate his or her judicial function over an issue in a case, the judge's neutrality is objectively in question; when this happens, the appearance of an impartial tribunal is in doubt, and the judge should take no further part in the proceedings.

And with that, Judge Morse granted the defense's motion disqualifying Wheel from participating in the Hunt case.[14]

Morse would later describe his decision to disqualify Wheel as "lighting the fuse." He knew that Wheel would be furious at the decision, viewing the disqualification as an embarrassment and a stain on her reputation. He was also fully aware by this time that Wheel had cultivated a strong personal relationship with Justice Hill, and that she was not shy about reaching out to him for help. Morse was also acutely aware that Hill was not beyond taking extraordinary steps to protect Wheel. He ordered the Hunt case set for trial. The tension in and around the courthouse was palpable.

A week before the Hunt trial was set to begin, Frank Fee called Morse and told him that Wheel's attorney, Louis Lisman, had just filed suit against him at the Supreme Court challenging his right to disqualify Wheel from the Hunt case. Morse would recall: "Fee asked me about service, which I told him I would waive. Nevertheless, Fee and the sheriff drove to my home and served me, Fee telling me Wheel didn't want to take any chances."

In addition to challenging Morse's right to disqualify her, Wheel also asked the Supreme Court for a stay of Morse's disqualification order so she could continue to sit on the Hunt case while the appeal was pending. Supreme Court rules provide that actions are filed with the clerk, who then distributes the filings to all the justices. Conferences are then held, issues debated, and decisions made. Not in this case. Wheel departed from the rules and took the extraordinary step of filing her petition solely with Justice Hill. Acting alone, and without even consulting the other justices, Hill immediately granted Wheel's request for a stay of Morse's disqualification order pending resolution of the appeal. Hill then personally went to the Chittenden courthouse and hand-delivered his decision to court clerk Fee to be sure he understood what had been ordered.

---

14    See Appendix A: Morse Opinion Disqualifying Wheel in *State v. Hunt*.

Morse was stunned. Hill had cited no authority for his actions, and there was no evidence any of the other justices were even aware of what he had done. Hunt's defense attorney strongly objected, and immediately filed a motion asking the full Court to reconsider the decision and to allow the Hunt trial to begin as scheduled. What followed next remains one of the darkest moments in the long history of the Vermont Supreme Court. On January 3, 1985, just seven days after Morse's decision disqualifying Wheel from the case, and without a request from or even notice to the State or to Hunt's attorneys, the Supreme Court ordered the Hunt case transferred from Chittenden to Lamoille County. The Court then declared Wheel's disqualification from the Hunt case moot and dismissed the case, thereby erasing the stain of disqualification from her record. Morse would later say that "*Wheel v. Morse* may hold the record for the fastest lawsuit to be decided by a supreme court. Well before the time I was allowed to file an answer, it was decided, opinion and all."

It was an extraordinary, unprecedented act of raw judicial power. Hunt's defense attorney, Robert Gaston, was outraged, noting that no one had requested a change in venue, and that the only issue before the Court was whether Judge Morse had the authority to disqualify Wheel. He reacted to the Court's order, "The Supreme Court acted without a hearing and in vio-lation of its own notice of hearing." Justice Wynn Underwood strongly dis-sented from the Court's order removing the case from Chittenden County, stating that the Court had "acted precipitously." Hill, who voted with the majority, denied that changing the venue of the case without a hearing was an effort to protect Wheel. Rather, he said, somewhat brazenly, it was an effort to solve a thorny dispute between two judges: "I've always been an advocate of side judges. I don't find them offensive."

In the spring of 1985 Governor Madeleine Kunin appointed Hayes to join Hill as a justice of the Supreme Court. Wheel decided to throw a big party to celebrate Hayes' appointment. She had reason to celebrate. She had demonstrated the remarkable power she wielded at the highest levels of the state's judiciary, and she would now have another close friend on the Supreme Court. Wheel hadn't spoken to Morse in months, and she didn't invite him to Hayes' party. Hayes stopped by Morse's chambers the day of the party and urged him to "come along." Morse politely declined, and would later say that "he wouldn't have been caught dead at it."

The events in the Hunt case, and the elevation of Hayes to the high court, only solidified Wheel's power and arrogance at the Chittenden courthouse, where Morse was left to wonder how these events could possibly have unfolded as they did. He would now be alone at the Chittenden courthouse with Wheel, and with both Hill and Hayes now on the Supreme Court, Morse would later tell colleagues that he felt he was "cooked." But as 1985 drew to a close, Wheel's arrogance and abuse of power would finally begin to catch up to her. Her life, and the lives of three Vermont Supreme Court justices who had come under her spell, were about to be changed forever.

## C. THE INVESTIGATION

While Assistant Judge Wheel remained close friends with Justices Hill and Hayes after their move to the Supreme Court, her power and arrogance had not made her many friends among the staff in her own courthouse. Rumors of personality clashes and difficulties there were rampant. One example of Wheel's pettiness and the tension it created is that she did not speak to Clerk Frank Fee for nearly a year because she was upset over where Fee had seated her at a Christmas party. Kim Sherman, a former deputy clerk at the court, described Wheel as hot or cold and said that her unpredictability was troubling: "Sometimes you'd say good morning to her, and she would walk right past you…. This isn't unique to me."

No one knew the source of the information flow from the Chittenden courthouse to the attorney general's office, but in late December 1985, word surfaced that the attorney general's office was investigating allegations that Wheel had improperly used county money to pay for Justice Hayes' celebration party, which had been held the previous March in the first floor jury room at the Chittenden courthouse. It was reported to have included food and an open bar and was attended by several judges and members of the local legal community.

Although Jeffrey Amestoy, Vermont's attorney general, refused to confirm the investigation, Chittenden County's state's attorney, Kevin Bradley, stated publicly that the attorney general was investigating the allegations against Wheel and confirmed that his own office was also investigating the matter: "I expect that we will sit down sometime with the attorney general's investigators to coordinate things." Bradley stated that interviews of courthouse personnel were scheduled to begin the following week. Amestoy did formally notify Chief Justice Allen that he was conducting an investigation into the allegations.[15]

---

15  See Appendix B: Amestoy Letter to Allen (Nov. 30, 1985)

Although Wheel refused to comment or respond to the allegations, other personnel in the courthouse seemed only too happy to discuss the matter publicly. Fee and his chief deputy, Diane Lavallee, described how a week after the party, Wheel had told them to withdraw $2,450 in cash from the county's passport fund to pay Forest Hills Restaurant, which had catered the party. Both Fee and Lavallee said that Wheel told them not to tell the county treasurer, John Fitzpatrick, what the money was for. Lavellee described how she went to Fitzpatrick's law office and Fitzpatrick signed the withdrawal slip. Fee told the local media that Wheel had made it clear to him that she did not want Charles Delaney, the other assistant judge, to know that she had ordered the bills paid for in cash. Fee said he told Wheel he would need a receipt for paying the caterer's bill and that he would have to show it to Delaney if he asked. Fee said Wheel replied that Delaney probably would never ask.

Delaney would later state that he had agreed to Wheel's request to sponsor the party for Hayes because she had told him it had been done once before in 1976, when Hill had been appointed to the Superior Court. Delaney made clear his limited role in the affair, saying, "I had nothing to do with planning the reception and I did not attend." Delaney reportedly told Fee that no more large bills were to be paid in the future without his knowledge. He also related that he had been attempting to talk to Wheel, but she has not been available, although both of them had been at the courthouse all week.

Fee made clear that the assistant judges set up policies in the court and it was up to him to see that they were carried out. Under normal circumstances, he said, both assistant judges would approve expenditures, but cash transactions required only one assistant judge's approval: "She brought Lavallee and me in here to my office and told us what we were going to do about a week after the party." As clerk, Fee said he had no choice but to get the money for Wheel, but added, "At no time did I intend to hide it."

As these allegations splashed across the local media, Wheel had remained silent, but a sign that public opinion about her was beginning to sour was not long in coming. In the Letters section of the local media, a citizen asked:

> Are judges from superior court accountable to no one? Can the superior court use public funds for private functions? How long has this been going on? Can a lady who professionally passes judgment on manners and morals consider

herself above the laws and traditions of Vermont? We need candid answers from Wheel, not continued arrogance.[16]

The letter appeared on the same day as news of a second investigation of Wheel hit the front pages of the local media, announcing that a criminal investigation was being conducted into allegations that Wheel had submitted pay vouchers for court work on days she did not sit on court cases and thus was not entitled to be paid. Assistant judges are paid a *per diem* for each day they hear cases. They submit their pay vouchers to the state each month, listing the days on which they worked in court. The local media had conducted an investigation and reported that it had checked in March 1985 for the 17 days that Wheel claimed in pay vouchers to have worked on court business and for which she was paid $906.10 (approximately $2,200 in current dollars). A review of computer entries showed that she did not sit on any cases during those 17 days. When computer records for the first 11 working days in April 1985 were also checked, they showed that Wheel did not sit on any cases during that period, but that she had submitted pay vouchers for those 11 days and was paid a total of $586.30 (approximately $1,400 in current dollars).

The computer records were based on court documents, including a daily calendar of cases to be heard before the judges and case files that included both notations on the file folder jackets of any action taken and the names of any judges who sat on the case. The computer records indicating which judge sat on a case, Fee said, are "99 percent accurate. The file is given to the docket clerk and goes onto the permanent docket card, which is now on a computer," and added, "Therefore, you can take at any time the cases heard on any given day and who heard them, and it will be on the file covers, and on the computer." Fee's account of the process was affirmed by Thomas Lerner, the administrator for the state courts, who stated, "The information based on the judges' notations is the register of official action and ought to reflect who participated in what and who didn't." Lerner also said that "as a matter of course, superior court judges will note for the record which assistant judges were there."

The two appointed judges assigned to the Chittenden courthouse at that time were also interviewed by the attorney general's investigators. Judge Morse reported that Wheel had hardly spoken to him since his decision disqualifying her in the Hunt case and that she never sat on a case

---

16  Letter to Editor, *Burlington Free Press*, December 21, 1985

with him during the March and April periods in question. Judge David Jenkins could not remember whether Wheel was present when he was presiding: "I just don't remember her not sitting for that length of time. But I can't say it's not true. The best record is the clerk's record."

The new president of the Vermont Association of Assistant Judges, William Collins, elected after Wheel had abruptly resigned the position a year earlier, also chimed in with a public comment. Collins, an assistant judge in Addison County, made clear that "[a] superior court judge has to be present for the court to be officially in session and for the assistant judge to get paid." A retired assistant judge from the Chittenden court, John Donahue, also observed, "The Supreme Court has been fairly stiff on what constitutes court work and would not recognize what I would call borderline things."

Although Wheel continued to remain silent in the face of the allegations and growing concerns, a few people close to Wheel came to her defense, saying publicly they strongly believed her to be innocent of the allegations and that it would only be a matter of time before she explained the "whole story." Esther Sorrell, a former state senator and a stalwart in the local and state Democratic Party, told the local media that Wheel "is very honest and very meticulous, and I think there's got to be more to the story than this." Another old-time Burlington Democrat and a former state representative, Sadie White, worked with Wheel on several election campaigns. She said she was surprised to learn of Wheel's alleged use of public money for a party for Hayes: "Oh God, I was dumbfounded. She's a well-educated person; she's never done anything underhanded before that I've known of. I do feel she is all wrong. There must be something, some answer to it."

Word soon spread that the attorney general's office had opened a formal inquest into the allegations of Wheel's alleged improprieties. An inquest, much like a grand jury, serves as an investigative tool in a criminal matter under investigation. The state initiates the request, and if granted, a judge oversees the investigative hearing. The judge's role in an inquest hearing is limited to issuing subpoenas, swearing in witnesses, and advising witnesses of their right against self-incrimination. The state may then decide to bring criminal charges if it concludes sufficient evidence exists to establish a crime has been committed.

On January 7, 1986, a day-long inquest was held in the Wheel investigation behind locked doors in a courtroom on the second floor of the state district court building on Pearl Street in Burlington. Inquests are held in secret, with witnesses ordered to maintain confidentiality as to the proceedings. The long, narrow window in the door to the courtroom was covered with paper, blocking anyone from looking in. Neither county state's attorney Kevin Bradley nor David Suntag, head of the criminal division of the attorney general's office, would comment on what transpired at the inquest.

In late February, word surfaced that Wheel had attempted to have veteran court reporter Joan Girard transferred out of the Chittenden courthouse. Girard, who had worked as a court reporter at the courthouse for five years, responded, "It's true," when asked if Wheel had urged a court official from Montpelier to reassign Girard to another court. Girard was careful not to comment on reasons why Wheel might want her out of the courthouse, but she did note that she was the only court employee to testify at the inquest the previous month looking into Wheel's alleged improprieties. Lee Suskin, who worked for the state court administrator's office, announced that instead of being transferred out of the Chittenden court, Girard would be re-assigned from Wheel's second floor courtroom to the third-floor courtroom to "ease tensions between the two." He said Girard would now work only with Assistant Judge Delaney.

Another employee, Deputy Clerk Margaret Malinowski, spoke publicly about the general level of tension and discontent among courthouse staff, relating that she and nine other court employees had been due a pay raise a month earlier but had not received it because Wheel had held up the budget, objecting to the increases that Fee had proposed. Malinowski said the employees had hired a local attorney to protect their interests in the budget hearings and were considering forming a union, but she added, "The raises are only a minor part of our concern. Things are a mess down there at the courthouse."

Although there continued to be no comment from Wheel on any of the allegations, several courthouse employees and members of the local bar began to speak out publicly about the role of assistant judges and the situation that had been created at the courthouse. Michele Millham, the receptionist at the courthouse, told local media that the turnover of employees had been extremely high, and many people feared for their jobs. "It's been real tense. Wheel has the power to either sign or not sign our pay vouchers," she said, adding that Wheel hardly ever entered the clerk's office, and would send someone else to pick up her mail.

Former Governor Phil Hoff, by then a state senator, and other members of the local legislative delegation met with court employees to discuss the problems at the courthouse. After the meeting Hoff noted, "They're talking about the impossibility of getting anything done, the impasse between the two judges, the low level of morale. It's an indication of their level of frustration. They don't know where to turn." Hoff said that Wheel's difficulties pointed to a person who had yet to learn how to handle power: "There's a suggestion that at least when she gets in a position of power, she carries things a little bit too far…"

A local editorial in March challenged Wheel on her silence in the face of the allegations. Noting the inquiry into the alleged improprieties was approaching three months in length, the editorial cited Wheel's obligation as an elected official to discuss and respond to the charges: "She cannot grant herself immunity simply by failing to appear at a budget meeting or refusing to answer telephone calls from the media. As a public servant, she owes the people who elected her an explanation." The editorial went on to suggest it might be time to put elected clerks in charge of courthouses: "When elected officials begin to believe that they are no longer accountable to the people, it is apparent that drastic steps are necessary to disabuse them of that notion."[17]

On April 23, 1986, an investigator from the criminal division of the attorney general's office served Wheel with a subpoena ordering her to appear at an inquest hearing to be held on May 6. There had been a lull in news about the investigation following the first inquest proceeding in January, and the news of the subpoena confirmed the state was actively moving forward with its investigation. As the inquest hearing was approaching, Wheel reported to the Burlington police that her desk at the courthouse had been burglarized and that papers that would have exonerated her from the pending criminal investigation had been stolen. A Burlington police detective who investigated the claim reported that Wheel said her desk had been pried open, papers were disturbed, and some papers stolen. Wheel told the detective that "correspondence" hand-written on three pages of yellow paper had been in the middle drawer of her desk and was missing. The detective wrote in his report that Wheel "said that the notes were pertaining to information that she gathered over a period of about four months. Judge Wheel said that it would be difficult to duplicate as it would take a long time to research."

---

17  Editorial, *Burlington Free Press*, March 9, 1986

The detective noted in his report that he found two distinctly different marks on Wheel's desk indicating that it had been pried open. Wheel explained that one set of marks was from an incident five days earlier when she accidently locked her purse in her desk. The second set of marks appeared newer. The court's maintenance man, Victor Fremeau, told the detective that he saw three doors ajar that Monday morning that he normally unlocks and opens. Another court employee, Fiona Farrell, said she heard keys jingling outside of her office and assumed it was the janitor. The story would become even more bizarre. The day after reporting the alleged burglary, Wheel telephoned Burlington Police Chief Kevin Scully and gave him the names of seven "suspects" she believed could have committed the burglary. These included Fee, retired U.S. Marshall Earl McLaughlin, Chittenden County Sheriff Ronald Duell, court reporter Joan Girard, court officer and former state trooper Bobby Jo Jackson, Burlington attorney Allen Bruce, and Kevin McLaughlin, a deputy sheriff.

When the detective asked Wheel in a follow-up interview why she had mentioned those individuals, Wheel told the officer that "they were players involved in some way in problems at the court. She said she believed that any one of them may know information about or may have actually taken the papers from her desk." When asked what she would say if someone accused her of prying open her own desk, Wheel offered that she had pried her desk open once after locking her keys in the desk. The detective's report noted that "Judge Wheel was evasive, did not directly answer the question posed and did not directly say that she did not pry open her own desk."

Asked to comment on being named a suspect in the alleged burglary, Fee said, "Being the county clerk and someone in charge of the building and staff, I'm not surprised." Others named as suspects declined comment, although Girard noted, "Among the lists of suspects is a former U.S. Marshall, the Chittenden County Sheriff, a former Chittenden County State's Attorney and myself, and I have a high-level FBI clearance. I believe this shows how preposterous this whole thing is." The event prompted Girard to have seven t-shirts made up with "The Wheelgate Seven" emblazoned across the front. Calls for Wheel to break her silence were growing. Her failure to show up at a county budget meeting, where the press had hoped to finally get a comment from her, only exacerbated the situation.

# D. THE JUSTICES GET DRAWN IN

In early May 1986 troubling details about the relationship between Wheel and Supreme Court Justices Hill, Hayes, and Ernest Gibson exploded into public view. Local media reported that Wheel had made 54 telephone calls from her home to the three justices since the start of the investigation. She had called Gibson at home 18 times and had made numerous calls to Hill. She made 16 calls to two Montpelier hotels, the Brown Derby and the Tavern Motor Inn, where Hayes stayed when he was in Montpelier. The longest call was reported to have lasted 97 minutes. One of the calls was to Hayes the evening of May 5, the night before Wheel was scheduled to appear at an inquest hearing. Hayes publicly acknowledged he had received calls from Wheel at the hotels, but he said the conversations were not inappropriate and that he never discussed the criminal investigation with her: "If she called me there, I would talk with her. She frequently had a number of things she was critical about." Assistant judges in other counties around the state indicated they rarely, if ever, called individual justices of the Supreme Court.

Another deeply troubling incident was reported involving a memorandum Hill wrote to the other members of the Supreme Court which redefined and substantially broadened the duties of assistant judges. It was written on December 30, 1985, just two weeks after the investigation into Wheel's pay vouchers had become public. The new definition, which Hill claimed that Justices Hayes and Gibson had worked on with him, cited the 'official duties' of assistant judges as:

> Attendance at a superior court when necessary to the advancement of the disposition of any action between litigants or at any function desirable or necessary to the operation or betterment of the Judicial Branch.

Justice Hill's memorandum went on to list certain actions that were not to be considered official duties, and listed several duties that could be considered as official, and then offered this guideline:

> We find that language cannot be precise enough to specify all the possible circumstances wherein assistant judges will have earned state compensation for having performed official duties for which an assistant judge would be paid. Some discretion therefore must be placed in the presiding

judge. The presiding judge, however, may accept representations of any person whose account he must approve.[18]

The new guidelines issued by the justices were seen as significant and
suspect, as a central aspect of the attorney general's investigation was
whether Wheel had performed official court duties on days for which she
had submitted pay vouchers. A month later, on February 3, 1986, Hill put
the new definition into effect in a memorandum sent to all of the state's
superior court judges.[19]

A week later, Chief Justice Allen wrote to Thomas Salmon, Chair of
the Judicial Conduct Board, and formally asked the Board "to investigate
allegations in the media" that Assistant Judge Jane Wheel had collected
fees for days when she did not attend court or engage in official duties.
The Chief Justice made it clear that his request constituted "a complaint
charging a violation of one or more acts of misconduct."[20]

As the Wheel investigation continued into the spring of 1986, another
deeply troubling report revealed that Justice Hill had written a letter to
Attorney General Amestoy expressing the "deep concern of the Court
over the time that has passed" since Amestoy had launched the Wheel
investigation. The letter, written on May 28, 1986, touched on two points.
It urged Amestoy to resolve the Wheel investigation as quickly as possible:

> Because suggestions of improper conduct upon the part
> of a judicial officer tend to cast a cloud upon the entire
> judiciary, we would request and urge that this matter be
> resolved at the earliest possible date consistent with the
> obligations imposed on your office.

The letter also expressed concern over leaks of reports of the secret
inquests that were being conducted by Amestoy's office:

> We are further concerned about the disclosure appearing in
> the media pertaining to an inquest in this matter. As this
> Court has indicated in the past, it is the policy of the law
> that secrecy is mandated in these proceedings. We assume
> that you have taken, or will take, appropriate steps to insure
> that such disclosures cannot be attributed to your office.[21]

---

18   See Appendix C: Hill Memorandum to Other Justices
19   See Appendix D: Hill Memorandum to Superior Court Judges
20   See Appendix E: Allen Letter to Salmon
21   See Appendix F: Supreme Court letter to Amestoy

It was reported that the initiative to send the letter, which was signed by Justice Hill 'For the Chief Justice,' was led by Justice Hill, and that it had created a considerable amount of disagreement and dissension among the justices. As remarkable as this letter was, it was even more disturbing that Justice Hill then went to the attorney general's office, hand-delivered the letter to Amestoy, and then sat and stared at Amestoy while he read the letter. Amestoy told Hill he would reply in writing, and would later testify that as Hill left his office, Hill turned to him and said "...words to the effect...that it would not be advisable to release this letter publicly."[22] When Hill was later asked about the letter's reference to leaks from the attorney general's office, Hill, apparently blind to the ethical implications of his actions, said "His [Amestoy's] office leaked this letter, so yes, I am concerned."

Governor Madeleine Kunin, who had appointed Hayes to the Supreme Court a year earlier, spoke publicly of her concerns. In saying at a news conference she had not lost confidence in Hayes, she asserted, "We don't have any hard evidence. We really have to count on the judicial system... I think people will separate, will have to separate, what's there by implication. We don't accuse people by innuendo." John Dooley, the governor's administration secretary, spoke publicly of the practical implications arising from the scandal and its impact on the judiciary: "The place that concerns me more personally is in superior court. That's a people's court. I can't imagine the thousands of people reading about this feel their legal problems are getting full consideration." Dooley further noted that "[t]he image of the Supreme Court is more correctable. I think the public view of the trial court in Chittenden County will not be the same for a long time."

The local media was also getting more agitated. Noting that "as plots go, the case of Chittenden County Assistant Judge Jane Wheel...grows more complex as time passes," an editorial opined that the public:

> ...must ask itself whether Hill and Hayes have committed serious breaches of legal ethics by their apparent attempts to intervene on Wheel's behalf. More important than her guilt or innocence is the larger question of the propriety of the judiciary. Judges, particularly Supreme Court justices, must set exemplary standards for themselves to avoid even the suspicion of misconduct.[23]

22   Amestoy testimony before the Judicial Conduct Board, March 9, 1988
23   Editorial, *Burlington Free Press*, July 18, 1986

Some lawyers and judges stated publicly that Wheel's relationship with Hill, Hayes, and Gibson had led to tension on the high court, occasionally pitting the three of them against Justice Louis Peck and Chief Justice Frederick Allen. It was especially disconcerting for Allen. "It's been a nightmare for him," said one trial judge who knew him. Justices Hill, Hayes, and Gibson had all been judges in lower courts and were considered judicial insiders, whereas Allen and Peck had come from outside the court system—Peck from the attorney general's office and Allen from private practice. Allen himself declined to comment, but Hayes acknowledged that there was occasional friction among the justices. "There are three people who came off the bench on the court, and two people who didn't," he said. "They don't always see eye to eye." For his part, Hill offered this comment: "As far as I know, the Supreme Court has put absolutely no pressure on anybody to do anything." Referring to the letter sent to Amestoy, Hill said, "The letter speaks for itself. We don't have hidden agendas."

Hayes was also forced to defend his decision to step down from the Supreme Court to hear a case in Chittenden Superior Court. The case, *Lisman and Lisman vs. Manchester and O'Neil*, involved a dispute between law partners over the break-up of a law firm. Louis Lisman was a long-time personal friend of Wheel's, who also performed legal services for her. The case came up for trial in July 1985, three months after Hayes had moved to the Supreme Court. The *New York Times*, which was following the Wheel investigation, wrote that investigators were looking into whether Wheel had told Hayes he had to hear the case as a debt owed to certain rich "Jewish friends" of the governor who had supported his nomination to the Supreme Court. Governor Kunin was outraged over the statement, calling it a "very unfortunate, bigoted remark."[24]

Hayes said he did not believe there was any impropriety in his sitting on the case. He took the case, he said, in part because he believed it could be settled out of court and he was confident in his ability to nurture such settlements. Hayes went on to explain that he had told Wheel when he left the superior court that he was planning to return to hear the case and that she had said, "Well, you'd better. If you tell Jane Wheel something, it's written in cement." Hayes reportedly bristled at any suggestion that he violated protocol by hearing the case or that Wheel wanted him to hear the case of

---

24  *New York Times*, January 29, 1987

her friend to influence the outcome of the proceedings: "I think Jane Wheel thought I was a good judge and a fair judge and I would like to think that was her motive," Hayes said. The *Lisman* case settled before going to trial.

## E. THE COVER-UP

Wheel's four year term was up in the fall of 1986, and the notoriety of the investigation had brought attention to the position of assistant judge. As the primary election drew closer, four candidates announced their intentions to run in the Democratic primary. Although Wheel remained silent as to her intentions, word leaked that she would seek reelection. Two of Wheel's old political friends, Elaine Charboneau and Sadie While, offered less than a ringing endorsement.

"She said she was running," said Charboneau, who was a state representative from Burlington. "If she's putting out petitions, I assume she's running…but maybe she'll change her mind before Monday," which was the deadline for entering the race. Sadie White, herself a former state representative, said that Wheel's husband Malcolm had told her that Wheel would seek reelection. "She's got a right to be a candidate if she wants to be," White said. "If people don't want to vote for her, that's their decision…I'm glad I'm not running in her shoes." Wheel's husband went door to door collecting the signatures necessary to get her on the ballot, but he would not confirm his wife was going to seek reelection. "You'll have to ask her," he said. He did add that she would make an announcement about her intentions by the filing deadline the following Monday.

The weekend before the filing deadline, editorials unleashed scathing opinions about the entire affair and all the characters involved. One editorial reviewed all the questionable instances and reported behaviors that had been unfolding for months and opined, "The public must ask itself whether Hill and Hayes have committed serious breaches of legal ethics by their apparent attempts to intervene on Wheel's behalf." The editorial made clear that the case had now grown well beyond Wheel:

> The Jane Wheel saga isn't really about Jane Wheel. It's about five people who are supposed to have a better grasp of right and wrong than the rest of us—the Supreme Court. It's also about the credibility of two former governors, an attorney general, and a judicial system that seems

more interested in covering up controversy than in uncovering truth.[25]

Readers were reminded that the symbol of America's justice is a statue of a blindfolded woman holding a balancing scale, and noted that: "The scale seems to be missing in this case, leaving us only with the blindfold."

It was into this political and public arena that, on July 21, 1986, the last day to file as a candidate for the primary, Wheel announced her intention to run for re-election. As she filed her petition seeking a fourth term as an assistant judge, she read from a written statement, "I am a candidate for re-election because I am innocent of all charges. I believe the people of Chittenden County will make the decision as to whether or not I continue to serve as assistant judge, not the disgruntled lawyers nor the head of a state agency or a state senator." In classic, defiant Wheel style, she was all in.

As the investigation into Wheel's alleged improprieties continued into the summer, more details of the farewell party for Hayes continued to trickle out. Justice Hayes told the local media that he had learned of his appointment to the Supreme Court while he was out-of-state and that when he returned to Burlington, he was extremely busy finishing up work and preparing to be sworn in to his new position. During that time, Hayes said Wheel told him, "We're going to have a party for you. We're going to ask the Chittenden County bar," to which Hayes said he responded, "Won't that be expensive?" Hayes said that Wheel responded, "Oh, there's always money available for that kind of thing."

The farewell party itself was described in considerably more detail than had been previously disclosed. Guests at the party told reporters the lavish affair included an open bar and a "bottomless pit" of shrimp. It was reported that there was so much brie cheese that employees took home leftovers. Wheel boasted that fruit was flown in from California. And it was learned that the party had been catered by a restaurant in the neighboring city of Winooski, where Judge Wheel's son was a chef.

Hayes stated that, after the party, he asked Fee how much it had cost and was told it was more than $2,000. Hayes said he was told the party had been paid for out of a fund which contained money from the processing of passports, and he told a reporter he asked Fee: "Is that proper?" Fee

---

25  Editorial, *Burlington Free Press*, July 21, 1986

was said to have responded, "It's been done," meaning it had been done before, and referring to Wheel's having thrown a similar party for Hill when he was appointed to the high court. Hayes said he knew the funds were not tax dollars and that he was under the impression that a precedent had been set for using the funds for that purpose.

Just as the public was trying to make sense of these new revelations, the investigation into Wheel's submission of pay vouchers took an important new turn. The attorney general filed an affidavit signed by its investigator, Randall Moran. Moran explained that records of court proceedings were kept on the front of each case file jacket, along with the names of the presiding judge and the assistant judges who were present for the case. The investigators had previously reviewed all the files that were on the court docket sheets from March 5 through April 12, 1985, and Moran stated in his affidavit that they had "found no record that Judge Wheel sat on any case during the above time period, and no record that she signed any orders."

Moran's affidavit continued by stating that Wheel had later told Lee Suskin from the court administrator's office that file jacket entries were so "messed up" that she and her husband had gone in on the weekends and corrected some of them. Based on this information, investigators looked at the case files again, and this time, as Moran stated in his affidavit, they found Wheel's signatures on several jacket files where they had not been when the investigators had looked earlier.

Investigators also found inside a jacket file two court orders with Wheel's signature on them that did not have her signature on them when the investigators had examined the files earlier. In one of those cases, Moran retrieved copies of the original order sent to the lawyers involved in the case, which led him to write, "Those copies do not have Judge Wheel's signature on it." David Jenkins, the presiding judge in that case, was in the habit of putting a squiggle mark under his signature when no assistant judge was present, and Moran stated in his affidavit, "The order that Judge Wheel allegedly signed in the file clearly shows that she signed the order through the squiggle mark."[26]

Based on the Moran affidavit, Judge Levitt, who was overseeing the inquest, had issued an order requiring Wheel to give handwriting samples to the attorney general. The order, known as a "non-testimonial identification order," is used by prosecutors to obtain handwriting samples, hair samples, or other types of identification evidence for comparison

---

26  See Appendix G: Moran Affidavit.

purposes. Such an order can be signed by a judge only if there is probable cause to believe a crime was committed and that the order will be of aid in determining who committed the crime. In response to the order, Judge Wheel had signed her name to 25 blank file jackets so the state could compare her signature to those now found on the case file jackets.

With the revelation of the Moran affidavit, the public learned for the first time that the investigation had broadened, and that the state was now looking into whether Wheel had gone into the courthouse after the investigation had begun and signed her name to file jackets to make it appear she had "worked" on those days. And to make matters much, much worse, at the last inquest hearing in July, when asked under oath about those signatures, Wheel had denied they were hers. Suddenly, the winds of the investigation had dramatically shifted. This was no longer a case focused on allegations of improperly using public funds, or even on the allegations of claiming pay for time she didn't work. It had now become a criminal investigation into whether Wheel had committed perjury by lying under oath when she denied the signatures were hers.

Justice Hayes did continue to express an unusual interest in the Wheel investigation as it evolved and deepened. In a memo in June 1986, Hayes wrote to Thomas Lerner, the Court Administrator, indicating that he had "just learned that a false swearing investigation directed at Judge Wheel is under way based in large part on an affidavit of Randy Moran." Hayes goes on to tell Lerner that he believed Lee Suskin, who worked for Lerner in the Court Administrator's office, was claiming that Judge Wheel told him that she had altered the jacket entries on certain case files. In the memo Hayes quizzes Lerner, "Do you know anything about this, and if so, what do you know about it and when did you find out about it?"[27]

These new revelations caused a stir among increasingly uneasy members of the Vermont bar. David Wilson, a Montpelier lawyer and a former state administration secretary under Governor Richard Snelling, offered these concerns: "Right now, people only have questions, they don't have answers. I think those of us who view the judiciary in high regard can only hope that at the time we do have answers, those answers are going to maintain our faith in the system." Allegations of Wheel's improprieties had first surfaced in December 1985. Nine months later, the growing chorus of demands that Wheel explain her actions had become deafening for those following the long and winding path of the case.

---

27   See Appendix H: Hayes Memorandum to Lerner.

In a motion filed in August 1986, Wheel finally broke her silence and offered a first glimpse of her response to the allegations. She attacked Attorney General Amestoy, charging that the investigation was being driven by her "political enemies" and was designed to "damage her reputation during an election year." She charged that the attorney general had leaked information about the inquest to the media and had deliberately allowed the Moran affidavit to become public, thereby violating the confidentiality of the inquest proceeding. She also alleged that Moran had told witnesses that he would "get" Wheel. In an explosive allegation not previously known, Wheel alleged that former governor Phil Hoff had met with Justice Hayes and told him Amestoy would drop his investigation of Wheel if she agreed not to seek re-election as an assistant judge. In her motion, Wheel asked Judge Levitt to disqualify the attorney general and his entire staff from investigating or prosecuting criminal charges against her.

Each charge added new elements of intrigue into already complex, tangled allegations, pulling in more players and drawing the judiciary and legal community deeper into the morass. Amestoy's deputy, Brian Burgess, adamantly denied that the attorney general's office had been involved in any leaks of information, "[C]ontrary to the allegations contained in the motion, records of telephone calls, Supreme Court office memoranda and one Supreme Court memo to the attorney general's office were not obtained through the attorney general's office." Burgess also said that he had specifically requested that the Moran affidavit be sealed but that Levitt had denied the request, a fact Levitt later confirmed, explaining that the affidavit contained no material subject to secrecy.

Amestoy returned from vacation and wasted no time adding his views in response to Wheel's allegations. Denying any political motivation behind the investigation, he said, "The motion to disqualify the attorney general's office is an effort to close off the investigation. I think her attorney is seeking what he believes to be in the best interests of his client, but the allegations are without merit." Amestoy also denied his investigator was out to "get" Wheel, saying, "I'm confident that there's no improper motivation on behalf of this office on this investigation. Randy (the investigator) did not know who Jane Wheel was before this investigation, and I still have never met her." Amestoy did comment at length about the allegation that he had met with Hoff to discuss the Wheel case. Amestoy confirmed that he and Hoff had met in early June at Amestoy's request to discuss the adverse impact the Wheel case was having on the judiciary. The two were concerned with the growing tentacles of the Wheel case and how those tentacles had already appeared to have entangled two, and possibly three, justices of the Supreme Court.

Amestoy strongly denied his meeting with Hoff was politically motivated. He said that when they met to discuss the investigation, he and Hoff were acting out of concern for the integrity of the judiciary. He would not comment on the specifics of their conversation, but when asked if he was "receptive" to the idea of dropping the investigation if Wheel agreed not to seek re-election, Amestoy said, ""First, if there is sufficient evidence to conclude that someone has committed a crime, that person will be charged. Secondly, no promises were ever made that the investigation would be dropped or altered." Amestoy did share Hoff's concern for the impact the case was having on the judiciary. As he put it, "I share the concern that I think all lawyers and citizens share that the judicial system be above reproach. It is painful to all of us…to see allegations that relate to members of the system."

Amestoy would later come to suspect that his meeting with Hoff was all a set-up. Shortly after the meeting, Amestoy was at the 100th anniversary of the Rutland Library. Amestoy was a hometown Rutland boy and was feeling quite relaxed when Leonard Wing walked by, leaned over, and said in a quiet voice, "Let's step outside." As Amestoy joined Wing on the lawn, Wing let Amestoy know that things were going to go very badly for him. He ripped into Amestoy for meeting with Hoff and for sending him to negotiate a deal for Wheel. He accused Amestoy of extortion and told him he had breached his own ethical obligations. As Wing walked back inside, Amestoy was left out on the lawn, stunned and speechless.

Hoff also acknowledged the meeting with Amestoy, although he said the characterization of the meeting by Wheel's attorney "is just wrong," He denied referring to himself as an "errand boy," as Wheel had characterized him in her motion, but rather, said he had been an "intermediary." Hoff stated that he and Justice Hayes were old friends and that he had talked to Hayes about the Wheel case because "I knew he was a friend and adviser of Jane Wheel." Hoff said that Hayes had advised him that he would talk about the suggestion with Wheel's attorney.

Pressed on the ethics of his own role in meeting with Amestoy and Hayes, Hoff said that he believed he was acting in good faith, and added, "You had the very distinct possibility of contradictory testimony by members of the Supreme Court…it would appear the press would have a field day with our judges and our court system…" Hoff was very concerned about how the scandal was impacting the courts, "One of the things I fought hardest for in my political career is the dignity of the courts." Hoff genuinely feared that unless the investigation was settled, alleged connections between Wheel and the Supreme Court could surface that could damage the Court and the judiciary.

Later, Hoff again talked about his efforts to get the matter resolved. "I really feel terrible," he said. "I must say I have known Jane Wheel for many years." He added that he "didn't have anything against Jane Wheel, except I was very concerned about her disruptive behavior here. I was concerned about the functioning of the court. My objective was to get her off the bench and get rid of her destructive influence that was on the court." He continued by saying that "[i]f everyone bought into that arrangement I suggested, all of this would not have come about."

There is little doubt that Hoff fully appreciated the damage the Wheel case had already had on the integrity and reputation of the Supreme Court and the judiciary and the potential it held for even more damage. And while his intentions may have been noble in trying to find a path to end the controversy, one could question the wisdom, and perhaps the ethics, of his decision to meet with Hayes. Hoff would later say that he was unaware when he met with Hayes that Wheel had retained an attorney to represent her in the matter and that, had he known that, he might have taken his proposal directly to her lawyer. In any case, as a former governor and then state senator, Hoff's concerns were deeply rooted and his effort was well-intentioned, albeit fruitless.

Wheel's attorney understood the center of gravity of the investigation had shifted, and, in a new motion, he asked Levitt to destroy the hand-writing samples that Wheel had earlier been ordered to give to the state. Wing referred to language in the non-testimonial order indicating it had been granted only for an investigation into whether Wheel had added her name to some of the file jackets, not to investigate a charge of false swearing, which was what the attorney general was now pursuing. It was a creative argument, but one without merit. Unlike a search and seizure case, where the fruits of an illegal search can be suppressed, the crime of lying under oath stands on its own. In other words, it didn't matter what the attorney general was investigating; Vermont law provides that "A person who, being lawfully required to depose the truth in a proceeding in a court of justice…commits perjury shall be imprisoned not more than 15 years and fined not more than $10,000.00, or both."

With the stakes in the case suddenly a lot higher, Wheel stepped up her push to have the attorney general's office disqualified from pursuing what she continued to characterize as a "politically motivated" investigation. She charged the attorney general with bias and unprofessional conduct and called on Governor Kunin to step in and appoint a special prosecutor to take over the investigation. "Judge Wheel moves to replace the present prosecutors with an independent investigative agency without an established record of bias and breach of the applicable codes of conduct," Wing argued, adding, "It is Judge Wheel's position that a disinterested prosecutor should continue to examine her judicial affairs and on the basis of that investigation make a true and timely decision regarding the filing of any criminal charges. She welcomes such an investigation."

Wing also argued that the attorney general should be disqualified from pursuing the investigation based on the conversation between Amestoy and Hoff. As Wing put it, "The mere fact that the attorney general approached Hoff to discuss the investigation and that he approached an intermediary to Judge Wheel and not her attorney is a violation of the attorney general's code of ethics and requires his disqualification." As a prelude to what was coming, Wing added, "The fact of those conversations will be established by live testimony during the motion hearing." Levitt had set a hearing on all the pending motions for August 12, 1986. When asked whether he intended to subpoena Amestoy and Hayes as part of his "live testimony," Wing responded, "I guess you'll just have to come to the hearing to find out."

Wing repeated the claim that the attorney general's office had leaked information about the investigation to the press. He cited more than a dozen articles from Vermont's two largest daily newspapers and wrote "These articles, all undeniably from sources within the attorney general's office, contain information far beyond the fact and scope of the investigation. They disseminated to the press the prosecutor's own belief in the strength of his case," which, Wing argued, violated the prosecutor's own code of ethics. The attorney general responded by reiterating his earlier argument that any attempt to disqualify his office was premature, that the matter was only under investigation, and as no criminal charges had yet been filed, there was no case from which to disqualify his office. "Intervention by the court into a criminal investigation by the executive branch of government is beyond the court's jurisdiction and in violation of the separation of powers," Amestoy wrote, noting that, "Nowhere in the constitution or in federal statutes had the judicial branch been given the power to monitor executive investigations before a case or controversy arises."

Governor Kunin, along with much of the rest of the state, had been watching as the case unfolded in the media, and she finally broke her silence by rejecting Wheel's formal request for a special prosecutor to take over the investigation. "I see no necessity for the executive branch to intervene," she said. "I do not see anything wrong with the existing process." The Governor also said that she had not lost confidence in Justice Hayes, whom she had appointed to the Supreme Court a year earlier. While expressing concern about press reports questioning Hayes' conduct, she still felt it was premature to draw conclusions: "We don't have any hard evidence. We really have to count on the judicial system." Like others, however, Kunin noted the importance of resolving the investigation: "The longer this lingers, the more it will lead to speculation."

In a new filing five days before the scheduled hearing on the pending motions, David Suntag, the lead prosecutor from the attorney general's office, responded to Wheel's latest motion by noting that most of the information Wheel claimed was leaked was available in the public domain and that Wing and Wheel had offered no evidence that it came from the attorney general's office. "She alleges that this office had released protected information to the press, yet her specific allegations fail to bear this out," Suntag wrote. Turning up the heat in an already overheated battle, Suntag urged the court to dismiss without a hearing Wheel's motion to disqualify the attorney general's office from pursuing the investigation: "There is no support for Judge Wheel's assertion that this office has released protected information to the press, and her counsel's motion to disqualify on this ground violates the Rule 11 requirement that counsel undertake reasonable inquiry to insure that a pleading is 'well-grounded' in fact." The rule also requires that a motion not be interposed for any improper purpose such as "to harass or to cause unnecessary delay or needlessly increase the cost of litigation." In some more litigious states, lawyers routinely throw Rule 11 motions back and forth at each other. The Vermont bar, however, has generally acted more civilly, and a Rule 11 motion, which is a charge that a lawyer is acting in bad faith, is not common. Amestoy's filing of a Rule 11 charge here reflected how frustrated and angry he had become over the allegations Wheel's attorney continued to make.

Within a day or two of the motions being filed, Wing reported that he had subpoenaed six people to testify at the upcoming motion hearing, including Hayes, Hoff, Amestoy, Moran, and two newspaper reporters, Leslie Brown of the Burlington Free Press and Debbie Bookchin of the

Rutland Herald, both of whom had written many detailed articles as the story had slowly evolved over the previous several months. Hayes acknowledged that he would honor the subpoena it if he received it, and when asked what he thought it was about, responded, "Given the nature of the names that have appeared on television—Hoff and myself—I assume it has something to do with my conversation with Hoff, but that assumption could be erroneous." Hoff also confirmed receiving a subpoena and appeared to agree with Hayes. "The thrust of the motion is to force the attorney general to disqualify himself, so obviously what they are looking for from me are the conversations between the attorney general and myself to see if there are any indications of bias," he said.

Suntag asked Levitt to quash the subpoenas issued to Amestoy and Moran, arguing that the court lacked the authority to issue the subpoenas. As neither a civil or criminal complaint had been filed, he argued, the court had no power to force members of the executive branch to testify about a pending investigation. "These subpoenas purport to compel the testimony of members of the office concerning the conduct of that investigation," Suntag wrote, adding, "Such questioning (of prosecutors and investigators by a suspect) is without precedent, and would seriously impede the state's ability to gather and preserve evidence, to obtain candid responses to inquiries, and eventually, to prosecute violations of the criminal law."

Both newspapers also vowed to fight the subpoenas served on their reporters. The executive editor of the *Burlington Free Press*, James Welch said "Essentially, our role here is to report the news and to inform people of the state of what's going on. It's not to serve as an arm of either law enforcement or an attorney for one of the witnesses at an inquest." Welch made clear the newspaper had no intention of revealing confidential sources. The *Rutland Herald* took a similar position, indicating that it would also attempt to quash the subpoena.

The lawyer for both newspapers, Dennis Pearson, confirmed that he was preparing a motion to quash the subpoenas, stating that "it is an accepted First Amendment privilege that no reporter should be compelled to reveal information unless the information has been shown to be necessary and relevant to an important issue in the case." Pearson also said other avenues of obtaining the information had to be exhausted first and added that, while there was no effort to hide anything, newspapers must react consistently to avoid having reporters turned into unwilling and unpaid investigators for one side or the other.

Levitt had initially scheduled the August 12, 1986 inquest hearing to address the issues raised in Wheel's first motion seeking disqualification of the attorney general's office. There had been several motions filed since then, and now, two days before the scheduled hearing, it appeared that a Supreme Court justice, a former governor, the attorney general, and two newspaper reporters would be required to appear as witnesses in her courtroom. Moreover, motions to quash some of the subpoenas had been filed, and a decision on those motions would obviously have to be made before the Tuesday hearing.

The day after receiving the motions to quash the subpoenas, Levitt decided to conduct a telephone hearing with the lawyers in the case before determining how to proceed. She arranged a conference call with both Suntag and Wing. A journalist with the local media just happened to be present in the courthouse that afternoon and Levitt allowed the reporter to listen in on the call. Levitt began by asking Suntag to summarize his arguments as to why the subpoenas should be quashed. As Suntag finished, Wing strongly objected to the telephone conference and informed the court that he had not even received a copy of the attorney general's motion to quash the subpoenas. Wing let his frustrations be known: "I'll do whatever the court directs, but I think we are being taken advantage of here." He also showed he was unhappy that the court was even considering the motions to quash the subpoenas: "It was my understanding that the court was going to assume jurisdiction," adding, "I spent about $400 on subpoenas."

The fact that Wing had not yet received his copy of the state's motion to quash the subpoenas presented a problem for Levitt. It would clearly be unfair if she were to rule on the motion without Wheel's attorney having received it. On the other hand, time was running out. Levitt concluded the conference call and directed the attorneys to appear in court for a hearing the next day. She made it clear that the hearing would not necessarily be limited to the motions to quash the subpoenas but might in fact also address other pending issues in the case.

It was a tense courtroom on Friday morning as the parties gathered to argue their motions. After Wing reiterated Wheel's claim that this whole case was politically motivated and that the attorney general's office should be disqualified from pursuing it, Suntag responded forcefully, "There is only one conclusion I can come to, and that is this is the most blatant attempt to interfere with an ongoing investigation." He added "The motion would have an irreparable damage to the state's ability to investigate the case." After both sides summarized the extensive arguments set forth in their written motions, Levitt was ready with her decision. She first denied Wheel's motion to have the attorney general's office disqualified and removed from the case. She accepted the attorney general's argument that as no charges had yet been brought against Wheel, Wheel's attempt to remove the attorney general from the investigation was premature and would violate the separation of powers.

With respect to the motions to quash the subpoenas, Levitt ruled that Amestoy and two of his staff members should not be required to testify about the attorney general's investigation in the case, and she again cited the separation of powers doctrine. It was another major defeat for Wheel. Wing, who had argued that "Judge Wheel's civil liberties are being violated because of the manner in which she is being investigated," said he was disappointed with the ruling but not surprised: "I suppose it means one, we could appeal it, or two, wait until Judge Wheel is charged with a crime to file the motion again."

Wheel did gain one small victory from the Friday hearing. She had asked Levitt to release the Moran affidavit on which Levitt had relied when she had issued the order compelling Wheel to give handwriting samples to the state. "One point does strike me," Levitt said from the bench, "Jane Wheel does have a right to challenge non-testimonial evidence, and whether it was done with probable cause." She ordered the affidavit supporting the order released to Wheel. Wheel's attorney saw this small victory as significant, as the affidavit had changed the course of this case, shifting it from pay vouchers and pay days to whether Wheel had added her name to the court files months after the fact in an effort to have it appear that she handled judicial matters on certain dates and then had lied about it. In the end, Judge Levitt resolved all the issues that had been scheduled for the inquest hearing the following Tuesday, and announced that hearing would be cancelled.

With the flurry of motions and memorandums now resolved, things again slowed down in the long, drawn-out investigation. Hoff made news again, this time for filing a motion seeking the disqualification of Wheel from hearing a divorce case his client had pending in Wheel's court. Citing the fact that Wheel had recently referred to him as a "political opponent in the county's democratic party," Hoff said that her disqualification was necessary to avoid a situation where her impartiality might be reasonably questioned. Phil Hoff had been elected governor in 1960, and reelected several times before retiring to practice law. He returned to politics in the 1980s to serve several years as a state senator from Chittenden

County, and was active in Democratic Party politics. It is not entirely clear where the rancor between Wheel and Hoff started, but she saw Hoff as a threat, and reacted accordingly. A few months earlier, Alan Bruce, a Burlington attorney, had filed a similar motion to disqualify Wheel from sitting on one of his cases. Bruce noted that Wheel had listed him as a suspect in the break-in she had claimed occurred at her office last spring. He alleged in his motion that Wheel had "exhibited certain personal bias and prejudice" toward him "which could affect her ability to act fairly and objectively."

As well, pressure was building on the attorney general's office to move the case forward. Noting that Wheel had been under investigation for nine months, an editorial opined:

> What should concern the public about the case is account-
> ability. Taxpayers...are entitled to know whether or not
> their money has been misused by a court official. That
> the investigation has been shrouded in secrecy during the
> nine-month period is bound to raise suspicions that offi-
> cials are reluctant to bring charges against Wheel.[28]

## F. THE JUDICIAL CONDUCT BOARD
## TAKES NOTICE

In late August, 1986, less than a month before the primary election, and with the attorney general's investigation of Wheel continuing to grind along slowly, the Judicial Conduct Board was continuing to watch and read the same media reports as everyone else. A month earlier, the Board's Chairman, Thomas Salmon, had given a surprisingly free-flowing inter-view about how the Board might handle the situation if ethical complaints were filed against the justices. Salmon, who had appointed Hayes to the superior court bench, made clear he would have to consider disqualifying himself if charges were ever brought against Hayes, based on his long friendship with the justice. Phil Hoff said he would expect that if any aspect of the Wheel case came before the Supreme Court, justices with personal ties to Wheel would disqualify themselves, adding, "I don't have a single doubt in the world that they would." Apparently, however, Justice Hill still had some doubts. He declined to comment, saying he would

---

28   Editorial, *Burlington Free Press*, July 18, 1986

make that decision "at that time." He added, "When the case comes up before us, then the decision will be made. I haven't thought about it."

It took less than a month following Salmon's comments for the Judicial Conduct Board to announce that it had commenced a formal investigation into the alleged conduct of Justices Hill, Hayes, and Gibson, as well as into Assistant Judge Wheel's conduct. Salmon immediately announced that he was disqualifying himself from any role in the investigation and named Richard Mallary, vice-chair of the Board and a former Vermont congressmen, to take charge of the case. In making his first announcement about the investigation, Mallary said the Board had decided on its own initiative to investigate allegations of misconduct against the three justices: "Based on the information the Board has received, we felt there was probable cause to believe that there might have been misconduct according to the rules of the Supreme Court." Most complaints against judges are initiated by citizens who feel they have been mistreated or not been treated fairly by a judge. The Board's initiation of this investigation on its own initiative was unusual, and reflected the enormous amount of publicity the attorney general's investigation had garnered over several months.

Within a week of Salmon's announcement, a second member of the Board, Edward Costello, announced that he, too, would remove himself from the Board's investigation into the justices' conduct. A former chief administrative judge, Costello noted that he occasionally sat with Wheel in Superior Court and was friendly with the three Supreme Court justices under investigation, so, he said, "I just didn't think it was appropriate" to participate in the investigation. The decision by Salmon and Costello to recuse themselves from the Board's investigation meant that the Supreme Court needed to fill two vacant seats on the Board so that the investigation could go forward. This presented a problem. Three of the justices were the subjects of the Conduct Board investigation, and were automatically disqualified from participating in the appointments based on a Supreme Court rule prohibiting a member of the Court from participating in any proceeding involving that judge's discipline. The two remaining justices, Chief Justice Frederic Allen and Justice Louis Peck, decided to disqualify themselves, citing the fact that they were sitting on the same court with the three justices under investigation and that they might be called to testify at the Board hearing. It was an historic moment, reportedly the first time in the state's history that a case had prompted the disqualification of all five justices of the Vermont Supreme Court. The *New York Times*, took notice of these developments, reporting that: "The allegations involving Vermont's highest court reach so deep into the state's legal community that the case has already required the establishment of a 'rump' Supreme Court."[29]

Chief Justice Allen appointed retired Chief Justice Albert Barney to serve as acting chief justice in the matter. Barney then appointed retired Supreme Court Justices Percival Shangraw and Wynn Underwood, and retired District Court Judges Lewis Springer and George Ellison, to sit on the case. These five acting judges, appointed for just one day and for the sole purpose of filling vacancies on the Conduct Board, met and appointed Bradford lawyer Harvey Otterman to replace Salmon as chair of the Board and District Court Judge Shireen Fisher to replace Judge Costello. Barney told the media, "We were appointed just to make those appointments. When the Board makes its report, it is possible the Court may do the same thing, but it may be that one or two of the present court will decide to sit on the case." It would become known as the "Special Supreme Court," and although its membership would morph somewhat during the course of the case, it would meet several more times to resolve issues growing out of this increasingly complex matter.

## G. WHEEL OUSTED AND THE HUNT CASE RETURNS

As the fall of 1986 arrived, with its annual mosaic of colors spread across the surrounding hills and valleys, attention turned to the primary election scheduled for the first week in September. Although Wheel had remained largely silent about her reelection, her campaign literature stressed her incumbency and apparent proprietary view of her office: "I am running for re-election to my office...because I believe I have made a significant contribution to the office." Addressing the controversy she had created over her views on child custody issues, Wheel stated in her campaign flyer, "The best interests of young children will often require that they not be uprooted from one household and then back again and again, leaving the child spinning like a top. This is what too often happens in cases of joint custody."

Two of her opponents, Elizabeth Gretkowski and Roz Payne, said that while they had several reasons for wanting to defeat Wheel, her position against joint custody in divorce cases was foremost. "I think her position is unfair and unjust," Gretkowski said, continuing:

---

29 *New York Times,* January 29, 1987

When parents are seeking joint custody, I feel as a judge
I do not have a right to tell them they cannot do that.
The two parents know what is best for a child, and I don't
think any judge in an uncontested divorce should deny
parents joint custody" if that is what they have agreed on.

Payne agreed, adding, "I think it is in the best interests of the child
to have contact with both parents when that's possible..." Another candidate in the race, Clarence Dubie, also favored joint custody, depending
on the circumstances of the case, "Children need guidance from both
parents if they can get it." And Joe Jackson, a court officer and one of the
"Wheelgate Seven" whom Wheel had identified as a suspect in breaking
into her desk earlier and stealing papers, was the only candidate to frankly
say he was running to get Wheel out of office.

Wheel continued to believe right up to election day that she would
not be hurt by the investigation and the controversies surrounding her. "I
think the voters are sophisticated enough to realize what this is," she said,
referring to the investigation as a "political attack." The polls had not been
closed long, however, when she got the first whiff of what the voters actually
thought about it. Early returns showed she had received only 79 votes in her
home ward, compared to 353 she had received there in the previous election.

It was the most expensive assistant judge race in the state's history,
with candidates reporting spending in excess of $2,000. In the end, the
voters re-nominated the incumbent assistant judge, Charles Delaney, and
elected Elizabeth Gretkowski to be the Democratic Party candidates in
November. Wheel came in dead last in the six-person race, losing not only
her home city of Burlington but every town in the county as well. "The
dark clouds of doubt hovering over Assistant Judge Jane Wheel's head
opened up Tuesday and washed away her hopes for a fourth four year term
on the bench," as the newspaper reported, further noting that it was what
"can only charitably be described as an embarrassing loss."

Never one to quit easily, Wheel's only comment was to not rule out
an independent bid for assistant judge in the November election, a comment that drew a quick response from local Democratic Party officials.
"I think the voters made a very clear statement and I don't expect her
chances would be too good," said Maurice Mahoney, local Democratic
Party chairman. The party's county chairman, Ben Truman, echoed that
sentiment, "I don't see any great mandate for her to do so."

In early September 1986, the Hunt case again made its way to the
Supreme Court. Hunt had been convicted of first degree murder after the

Supreme Court had unilaterally ordered the case transferred to Lamoille County, without notice to the parties, in order to solve the Morse/Wheel "problem." Hunt had appealed his conviction, and one of the issues in his appeal was a challenge to the Supreme Court's authority to transfer the case to Lamoille County, an issue that directly involved Wheel.

The state was represented in the appeal by Assistant Attorney General Susan Harritt. Hunt was represented by William Nelson from the defender general's office. Nelson had asked Harritt to give some thought as to whether the attorney general's office should disqualify itself from the Hunt case, citing the *ex parte* communication Wheel had had with then Attorney General John Easton when Easton was running for governor. Nelson told Harritt that information made public about the investigation had revealed "frequent contacts between Judge Wheel and Justices Hill, Hayes and Gibson, along with the possibility she may have exerted improper influence." Nelson argued that he could be excused "for suspecting that Wheel applied directly to Justice Hill and Justice Gibson, both longtime associates with whom, it now appears, she is in the habit of communicating directly concerning court business." He told Harritt that "I don't want to contribute to this publicity storm and I'm letting you know beforehand so you will have a chance to consider the issue and take whatever action you feel appropriate."

Harritt disagreed that the attorney general office had a conflict of interest, but acknowledged that it was possible that an appearance of a conflict existed. She told Nelson the attorney general's office would withdraw as counsel from the Hunt appeal. Harriet filed a motion with the Supreme Court to withdraw from the Hunt case, and after discussions with Nelson, she wrote to him with her understanding of their agreement. The attorney general's office would continue to assist the new attorney, State's Attorney Terry Trono, and continue to play a limited role in the appeal. Harritt went on to describe the nature of the "understanding" between the attorney general's office and the defender general's office:

> "We understand that you are not and will not be filing a motion to disqualify this office from participating in the appeal, given our more limited role. You further indicated that you will not raise any other claims at this time or in the future regarding participation in the appeal by this office. Please let me know if you disagree with my statement of our mutual positions on this matter."

Nelson was a very experienced criminal defense attorney who often argued cases before the Supreme Court. He correctly sensed a need to be cautious when he replied to Harritt, "Yes, I agree with what you say in your letter," he wrote, but he added, "I do want to make clear, however, that I am merely acquiescing in this arrangement, and that my acquiescence does not signify approval. I think you (the Attorney General's office) should be off the case completely."

By this time Hill, Hayes and Gibson knew they were under investigation for misconduct by the Judicial Conduct Board based on their alleged interactions with Wheel. They also knew that the issue of the Supreme Court's transfer of the Hunt case form Chittenden to Lamoille County directly involved Wheel. Justice Hayes had been diagnosed with lung cancer a few months earlier, and he had left the bench to go into treatment. Both Harriet and Nelson would have been justified in assuming that Hill and Gibson would recuse themselves from hearing this motion. There was no doubt tension in the air as the justices filed into the hallowed courtroom of the Supreme Court, and the tension only increased when Hill and Gibson took their seats to hear the motion

Harritt went to the podium first and explained that, while the attorney general's office did not agree with Nelson that there was a conflict, "we do feel that there is a public perception of impropriety, or an appearance of impropriety by continued involvement on the part of the attorney general's office." Harritt then tried to explain the arrangement her office had with Nelson: "While recognizing the potential for conflict, the attorney general's office did not feel that we were precluded from providing legal research to Mr. Trono, who is now part counsel of record in this appeal." Justice Gibson was the first to interrupt with a question. In the soft, gentle voice for which he was known, Gibson asked Harritt, "I'm not sure, do I understand you? You're going to be partly in and partly out?" Harritt's immediate response was, "Well, I'm not trying to do that, I think that would be illegal." As Harritt further tried to explain that the attorney general's office would only be supplying the new attorney with research in the case, Justice Hill interrupted her, "How can you do that, without being half in or half out?" When Harritt tried to explain that the attorney general's office provides help to state's attorneys in lots of cases in which they don't even know the name of the case, Hill angrily shot back "You know the name of this case."

What ensued would later be described by observers as the harshest questioning of a lawyer in the Supreme Court chambers in years. While a recording of the hearing fully captures the harsh, angry tone and emotional bursts from Justice Hill, they can be gleaned from excerpts from the transcript. Hill first challenged Harritt on why this motion to withdraw was being made at this late date in the case.

> Hill:         You didn't know anything about the background of the case and the possible conflict of interest until Nelson told you about it?
>
> Harritt:    Well, your honor, today we don't believe there is a conflict.
>
> Hill:         Then why are you withdrawing?
>
> Harritt:    We have indicated that we believe there may be an appearance of...
>
> Hill:         What appearance, Miss Harritt? It is understood in the paper, by the way, that other people besides Judge Wheel are being investigated, does that include this Court so you want disqualification from some of us?

Harritt, herself a skillful, veteran prosecutor, attempted to deflect the attack, telling Hill that she was not involved in the Wheel investigation and had not read the newspaper articles.

> Harritt:    My intent in filing the motion and setting forth the scope of my participation in this appeal was to let the Court determine whether it was proper for the attorney general's office to participate in this appellate cause.
>
> Hill:         So if we think it's proper you will continue to represent the State?
>
> Harritt:    Well, the Court obviously has leave to grant the motion or not, so it's certainly up to this Court.

Justice Peck, one of the two untainted justices in this sordid affair, asked Nelson whether this motion arose out of something Nelson brought to the attorney general's attention. As Nelson answered in the affirmative, Justice Hill pounced again:

> Hill:         With which member of the AG's office, Mr. Nelson?
>
> Nelson:   With Ms. Harritt and also with Mr. Suntag
>
> Hill:         With Mr. Suntag?

| Nelson: | As well, yes. |
|---|---|
| Hill: | He has something to do with the Hunt case? |
| Nelson: | No, but we felt that there was a conflict between the State's role in the Hunt case and its role in the investigation of Judge Wheel. |
| Hill: | And you think that Judge Wheel has something to do with the Lamoille County Hunt case? |
| Nelson: | Yes, we feel it does, your Honor. |

Hill then jumped to the same question he had asked Harritt:

| Hill: | What about the members of this Court's participation, Mr. Nelson? |
|---|---|
| Nelson: | Well, it's difficult to know, and frankly, it's a decision that I will have to reach at some point. Whether before argument on the merits of this case, I might move to disqualify Your Honor, and perhaps other members of the court. That's a decision that... |
| Hill: | You can't make that decision now? There are more facts you need? |
| Nelson: | I don't have to make that decision now. |
| Hill: | We're sitting in this case. |
| Nelson: | That's correct. |
| Hill: | You're asking us to sit in this case, and you think that we're qualified now, but we may be disqualified at some future time. |
| Nelson: | I have not made the motion here, and I have, therefore, waived the issue. Whether it would be appropriate prior to argument of the merits is a decision that I will have to reach at that point. |
| Hill: | Do you think there is a difference between today and the argument on the merits? |
| Nelson: | I think there is, yes. |

Nelson was allowed some time to connect all the dots between the Hunt case and the investigation of Wheel. Then Gibson, still troubled by the attorney general's request to be half in and half out of the case, broke in again.

| Gibson: | What about Ms. Harritt's suggestion that their offices continue to provide some assistance in the case? |
|---|---|
| Nelson: | Your Honor, that is a position we have agreed not to contest. |

Gibson:    How can an attorney, once he or she has with-
           drawn, how can they then continue to act, espe-
           cially if the basis of the motion to withdraw is an
           appearance of impropriety?

Nelson:    I think I can say this much without violating my
           agreement with the attorney general...

Hill interrupted and pounced hard on Nelson.

Hill:      Do you have a secret agreement?

Nelson:    No, we don't have a secret agreement, but we did
           come to terms...

Hill:      Do you have a confidentiality between the two of
           you?

Nelson:    No.

Hill:      But why did you say what you said "without vio-
           lating my agreement." Don't you think this Court
           should know about any agreement you have with
           the Attorney General?

Nelson:    Certainly, and I will spell out the agreement we
           have reached.

After Nelson explained the understanding that the defenders general's
office and the attorney general's office had reached in the case, Justice Hill
attacked again.

Hill:      You don't believe there are any (Ethical Canons)
           that you have violated, Mr. Nelson, in making such
           an agreement?

Nelson:    That was a matter of concern with me, Your Honor.

Hill:      Is it still a matter of concern to you? And it is cer-
           tainly ethical on your part? And you think ethical on
           their part?

Nelson:    I think it's a borderline issue. I don't really know

Hill:      How borderline, Mr. Nelson?

Nelson:    To put it in the words I put it in my correspondence
           with Sue Harritt, I acquiesced in their continuing...

Hill:      You didn't advise this Court, did you? You acqui-
           esced in something, never advised this Court, and
           we had to drag it out of you before you advised this
           Court

Nelson:    I don't feel I have done anything improper, Your
           Honor.

Hill:      You acquiesced? The word you used is acquiesced?

| Nelson: | That's precisely the word I used. I acquiesced in it.... If I made the wrong decision, I apologize... |
| Hill: | It's not a matter of apology, Mr. Nelson, it's a matter of ethics. |
| Nelson: | I don't feel that I've violated the Canons of Ethics. Yes. In light of your perception that I've been covering up. I don't feel that I have. |
| Hill: | You don't think it's more than a perception? |
| Nelson: | No, I don't, Your Honor. |

After the hearing, Nelson said he was shocked by the tone of Hill's questioning. "I never saw anything like it," he said. He also said he was now "definitely considering" filing a motion requesting some members of the Court recuse themselves from the Hunt appeal on account of their ties to Wheel.

# PART TWO

*Criminal and Ethics Charges*

## A. WHEEL FACES CRIMINAL CHARGES

It had been over nine months since Attorney General Amestoy had opened an investigation into the allegations against Wheel, and by September 1986 public pressure was mounting on him to conclude the investigation. Editorials were harshly critical of the delay, with one noting that "Wheel has been turning slowly in the wind for nearly a year" and that it appeared "Amestoy is no closer to filing formal charges than he was weeks after the investigation started. Surely adequate information should have been collected by now to provide Amestoy with sufficient information to determine what course he will follow." Even the attorney general's competence was being questioned:

> What Amestoy has done since last November is inexcusable and creates the impression his office is being run in a slipshod manner…Failure of the Democrats to oppose Amestoy in the November election is a discouraging development since it guarantees that there will be little improvement in the attorney general's office in the next two years.[30]

Whether it was the public scolding and pressure the attorney general was receiving, or whether it was just time, on Tuesday, October 31, 1986, the attorney general's office formally charged Assistant Judge Jane Wheel with six felony counts of perjury for lying under oath during the earlier inquest hearings. In an affidavit laying out the charges, Suntag stated that Wheel had denied under oath she had altered court file folders, but that testimony of expert handwriting witnesses indicated she had, in fact, added her name to several file jacket folders. Wheel became the first Vermont judge to be charged with a felony. If convicted, she faced a maximum of 90 years in jail and a $60,000 fine.

The Moran affidavit that was filed in support of the charges offered more insight into the evidence supporting the criminal charges. Victor Fremeau, a maintenance man at the Chittenden courthouse, had testified at the inquest that Wheel had asked him to fetch several court file folders and that she had asked specifically for folders from cases during the timeframe in which she was being investigated. Fremeau was quoted as saying, "The *Burlington Free Press* said it was looking at the thing in March and

---

30   Editorial, *Burlington Free Press*, September 11, 1986.

April, whether she hadn't been there, and she wanted to see those files." The affidavit went on to state that Fremeau brought 20 to 40 case files to Wheel over a 10-day period in January or February and left them with her until she told him to return them.

The affidavit also noted that Suskin told Moran that during his investigation into the large backlog of cases at the Chittenden court, Wheel had told him she would often go into the courthouse with her husband on Saturdays to try to straighten out the court file folders that were in "a sad state." The Moran affidavit alleged that Wheel told Suskin that "she and her husband has had to go in on weekends and correct some of the jacket entries on the files." At the inquest, however, Wheel had testified that she never altered file folders or changed jacket entries. Attached to the affidavit were transcripts of Wheel's inquest testimony:

Suntag: Was there ever a day or a weekend in 1985 or 1984 when you went to Chittenden Superior Court to correct some jacket files?

Wheel: Never. Never wrote on a jacket.

Suntag: You never wrote on a jacket?

Wheel: Not to correct anything at any time. Reviewed them on the advice of my attorney. I reviewed them to get the consensus I spoke about earlier, but to change, to delete, to add, never.

In another affidavit accompanying the criminal charges, Suntag wrote that at an inquest hearing a week later, he had again asked Wheel about whether she had written on file jacket covers:

Suntag: And again, I think you told me that you didn't actually make any changes or mark anything?"

Wheel: I never touched the jackets. I would never alter. I'm a woman of integrity. I would never alter a jacket.

The Moran affidavit went on to state that Edward Smith, a document analyst with the U.S. Postal Inspection Service Crime Laboratory, had determined that on four jacket files, Wheel's name had been written by her. Smith also identified as being the judge's signature the "Judge Wheel" written through a squiggle mark on a court order.

Wheel appeared before Levitt for arraignment on October 1, 1986, and she pleaded not guilty to all charges. She was released without bail on the condition that she not touch any court files without first consulting the attorney general's office. As Wheel emerged from the courthouse, her attorney informed reporters: "The judge is not going to answer any questions." Suntag said after the arraignment that, "These are the only charges we have. We do not expect to file additional charges." He discounted criticism that after a ten-month investigation, Wheel was being prosecuted on charges of her alleged cover-up effort, not on the original allegations. Said Suntag in response, "We have filed charges. They are obviously quite serious charges. Other matters that are being investigated will come out in relation to those charges."

The day after Wheel's arraignment, Chief Justice Allen announced that the Supreme Court would meet to decide whether to suspend Wheel from sitting on the bench. "The disciplinary rules provide that we may suspend a judge that has been charged with a felony," Allen said, adding, "I am certain we will be meeting in the near future to make that determination." The rule calling for the suspension of a judge charged with a felony provided that the suspension be "with pay." Assistant judges, however, are only entitled to compensation when they are present in court and actually sit on cases. As Wheel was being suspended and would be ineligible to sit on cases, it meant she would not be compensated during her suspension.

Acknowledging the concern that three of the justices were friends with Wheel and themselves under investigation by the Judicial Conduct Board, Allen said it would be up to each of the justices to decide whether to remove himself from the deliberations concerning Wheel's possible suspension. Justice Hayes, who was still in treatment for lung cancer, had announced he would disqualify himself from any proceeding concerning Wheel. Justice Gibson said he would not disqualify himself: "I don't know of any reason why I should. I don't know that merely the fact that they're investigating or looking into some aspect of our relationship means I'm necessarily disqualified." Justice Hill refused to comment on whether he would participate, and as the hearing date drew closer, news reports suggested that Hill "apparently will not disqualify himself" from the hearing. Court Administrator Thomas Lehner reported that, as of Friday afternoon, Hill had not filed a motion to recuse himself and indicated that it would be difficult to find a justice to replace Hill in time for Monday morning's hearing.

On Monday morning, October 6, 1986, Justice Hill and Justice Gibson were indeed on the bench to hear arguments on whether Wheel should be suspended from the bench. The hearing was brief, with Justice Hill voting along with the other justices to suspend Wheel. However, Justice Hill strongly argued that she should be compensated during her suspension, and he managed to persuade Gibson and two of the other justices. It was, however, too much for the chief justice to stomach. The Court's opinion ordering Wheel's suspension was short, and Chief Justice Allen made his view known:

> 1. Assistant Judge Jane L. Wheel is suspended from acting in any judicial capacity until further order of the court.
>
> 2. In order that the provisions of Rule 5(1) providing that such suspension be "without loss of compensation" be fairly implemented, it is directed that Judge Wheel be paid judicial *per diem* compensation for each of those days certified by the Presiding Judge of Chittenden County that the business of that court authorizes the participation of assistant judges.
>
> ALLEN, C.J., concurred with paragraph 1, dissented to paragraph 2.[31]

The editorials criticizing Amestoy's handling of the investigation had clearly touched a sensitive nerve. With criminal charges now filed, Amestoy responded forcefully to the editorial criticism of his handling of the case. Writing in an op-ed piece, he quoted the 19th century English statesman, Benjamin Disraeli, who once observed that "one must not resent criticism, even when for the sake of emphasis it departs from the truth." Good advice, Amestoy noted, "but then again, Mr. Disraeli was never the subject of a *Burlington Free Press* editorial."

Amestoy went on at considerable length to explain the complexity and time-consuming nature of white-collar-crime investigations, noting that even when undertaken by federal authorities with more resources and laws, it was not unusual for investigators to take from 13 to 19 months or longer to conclude an investigation. He ended with this parting shot:

> "For those who look to the editorial page for guidance in evaluating public officials, your colleagues at the *Barre-Montpelier Times Argus* recently suggested 'thoroughness, persistence, competence and fairness'. I believe thoughtful readers will find that criteria more in keeping with Vermont standards than the 'opinion first, facts later' style of the *Burlington Free Press*."[32]

---

31   *In re Jane Wheel*, 147 Vt. 647 (October 6, 1986)

32   Op-Ed, *Burlington Free Press*, October 2, 1986.

Alan Overton, president of the Chittenden County Bar Association, commented that the lengthy investigation had been "disruptive and difficult" for county lawyers, who had to provide clients with complicated explanations of their court status. "I know from talking to other members of the bar that everyone is anxious to get this whole thing behind us...because it's embarrassing and it's difficult." Richard Mallary, acting chair of the Judicial Conduct Board, was unsure how the criminal charges would affect the Board's investigation. He noted that the criminal charges could force the Board to suspend its investigation of Wheel until those charges are resolved: "I would be less than candid if I didn't say that obviously this is going to have some affect—and I'm not sure what it should be." He went on to note that: "You have two formal procedures...dealing with the same issue. Whether there would be a potential conflict between one and another, I frankly don't know."

With Judge Wheel now formally charged with six felonies, the investigation shifted from an inquest over some alleged improprieties into a serious and complex criminal case. Wheel's attorney requested a list of witnesses and documents that the state intended to use at trial, and it provided a first glimpse into the size and scope of this case. The state listed twelve district and superior court judges as potential witnesses, along with all five Supreme Court justices, among the total of 122 potential witnesses. Documents included photographs taken at the party for Justice Hayes, expense forms signed by Wheel, and the letter Justice Hill had written and hand delivered to Attorney General Amestoy expressing concern over the length of time the Wheel investigation was taking, and over leaks that the letter implied were emanating from Amestoy's office.

Wing filed a motion requesting that Levitt disqualify herself from presiding over Wheel's criminal trial. He argued that Levitt's role in two secret inquest hearings, which were the basis for the charges against Wheel, might create problems and indicated she might be called as a witness in the criminal case. Based on Wing's motion and request, Levitt announced she was disqualifying herself, and District Court Judge Francis McCaffrey was assigned to hear the criminal case. McCaffrey ordered the case moved to Rutland District Court, where he was the presiding judge.

At a hearing in late December 1986, the attorney general's office added the names of 20 more potential witnesses and identified more than 50 memos, files, letters and other documents to be used as evidence. Levitt appeared on the supplemental list of potential witnesses for the state. Another new name on the supplemental witness list was Mary Kehoe, who had been a law clerk for Judges Hayes and Morse at the Chittenden court. In an earlier interview, Kehoe had described how she had arrived at the courthouse one day and found that overnight her office had been moved upstairs. "It was quite a shock to open up my office door and it wasn't there," Kehoe said. Observers said Wheel precipitated the move partly because of Kehoe's friendship with Morse, to whom Wheel had continued to refuse to speak after he had disqualified her from hearing the Hunt case.

After the perjury charges had been filed, legal observers had wondered why the attorney general had not charged Wheel with crimes related to the misuse of public funds or falsifying pay vouchers, the allegations which had started the investigation. Many of the documents filed with the attorney general's supplemental affidavit did relate to the initial allegations against Judge Wheel, offering a glimpse as to how the prosecution intended to present its case. These documents raised the question of whether Wheel's close personal relationship with Hill and Hayes, and to a lesser extent with Justice Gibson, represented undue influence in the judicial system, and whether normal court procedures had been violated.

Wing asked Judge McCaffrey for a delay in order to conduct more discovery. The judge expressed concern from the bench about the slow pace of the case: "I do feel there is some urgency to this in connection with Mrs. Wheel's right to a speedy trial." Wing responded by formally waiving his client's right to a speedy trial, saying publicly that McCaffrey "is concerned about Judge Wheel's constitutional right to a speedy trial. I'm concerned about Judge Wheel's constitutional right to a fair and impartial trial. I think it's far more important that we get these problems settled."

As 1987 dawned and the Wheel trial inched closer, Wheel's attorney made a new and somewhat startling charge. Wing alleged that Assistant Attorney General Suntag, who had been the lead prosecutor throughout the investigation and inquest and was now the lead prosecutor in the criminal case, once had a personal relationship with Judge Levitt, who had presided over the inquest. Wing attacked Suntag for failing to disclose the relationship, charging that it had cast doubt on the entire inquest proceedings. Levitt declined to comment publicly on the allegation, saying she was no longer involved in the case, although she did note that she had been assigned the inquest proceeding by the chief administrative judge, Stephen Martin. Suntag said he was not surprised by the charge and was "not particularly troubled." He said Wing had threatened to release the accusation if the attorney general's office did not drop the charges against Wheel and commented that "It's not unusual for a prosecutor to be personally attacked by a defense attorney and try and intimidate him into some kind of action. I've seen that before."

Wing again asked Judge McCaffrey to disqualify the attorney general's office from prosecuting the criminal case, raising several of the same arguments about "bias" and political motivation he had made during the inquest investigation. This time, however, Wing went after the Attorney General personally, noting that the Wheel investigation coincided with the attorney general's unopposed re-election bid: "No doubt Amestoy's unopposed and successful re-election effort was buttressed by the scurrilous details the attorney general garnered by the new media." It was evidence of how nasty the entire matter had become. Wing also went after Amestoy for allegedly approving Hoff's meeting with Hayes in an apparent attempt to resolve the Wheel case. "There is a strong appearance that Attorney General Amestoy would have been willing to quash the investigation if Judge Wheel consented to not running for re-election," Wing wrote, arguing that "…the idea amounted to a violation of defendant's civil rights and borders on extortion."

Finally, in a new argument, Wing maintained that information gained from the inquest hearings should be suppressed because Wheel had not been allowed to have counsel present during the hearings. Citing a recent opinion by another district court judge, Wing argued that because an inquest involves testimony, a witness has a legal right to counsel at the hearing. Inquest hearings had always been considered investigative in nature and witnesses had not been allowed counsel in the courtroom, although they could pause during the proceeding and consult with counsel at any time.

In responding to Wing's allegations, the attorney general's office made clear for the first time that even though Wheel was not charged with a crime with respect to the money she used for Hayes' party or for her pay vouchers, prosecutors intended to prove that Wheel collected state pay for days she did not do court work. Suntag explained that "Wheel's submission of those pay vouchers provided her with a motivation to alter court documents in an attempt to make it appear that she had, in fact, sat on cases during those days…. Those alterations, in turn, provided her with a motivation to lie under oath while testifying during two inquests." Suntag also dismissed the allegation that his prior relationship with Levitt had tainted the inquest proceedings. He noted that Wheel's motion merely stated that he and Levitt had had a relationship which ended at least two years before the inquests at issue here, and he argued that Wheel failed to show how his "so-called" relationship with Levitt prejudiced Wheel's rights at the inquest. "Without something further," Suntag said, "Judge Wheel's motion to invalidate the finding of probable cause is inadequate as a matter of law." Judge McCaffrey advised the parties that he would schedule a hearing in April to hear all of Wing's pre-trial motions. He denied Wing's request to subpoena Amestoy, Suntag, and two of their assistants to appear at the hearing, noting that relevant case law did not favor prosecutors being called as witnesses by criminal defendants to inquire into their motives. McCaffrey found that "there have been no affidavits, depositions, sworn statements or any other factual materials presented to require such an interrogation."

In mid-April 1987, in a battle that would last three days, the lawyers argued all the pre-trial motions covering most of the preliminary issues over which the parties had been wrestling for months. Much of the April hearing was taken up by the testimony of Kevin McLaughlin, a deputy sheriff in Chittenden County; Francis Fee, the Chittenden court clerk; and Randall Moran, the investigator from the attorney general's office who had done most of the work constructing the case against Wheel.

Deputy Sheriff McLaughlin started out by describing how one evening in late 1985 he received a call from Frank Fee, a friend whom he knew from being around the Chittenden courthouse. Fee seemed anxious and asked McLaughlin to meet him in a Burlington parking garage after work one night. There Fee told McLaughlin he had something he wanted to show him. He opened his trunk and began pulling out copies of Wheel's pay vouchers and a journal he had been keeping on Wheel's attendance in court. The notes and records showed that Wheel had submitted pay vouchers for several days when she was on vacation in Florida and several other occasions when she was not in court. Fee had kept records and notes of it all. He told McLaughlin he trusted him and did not know what to do. McLaughlin testified that he advised Fee to leave all the documents in his trunk and to give him a few days to figure out how to best handle the situation. McLaughlin initially went to his boss, Sheriff Butch Duell, who told McLaughlin he should delay acting on this information, as Wheel was preparing to run for reelection and the information would be explosive. McLaughlin believed he had an obligation to report the information and he told Duell he was uncomfortable with any delay. McLaughlin then went to Montpelier to meet with Attorney General Amestoy and described the information Fee had collected. Amestoy assigned Randall Moran, an investigator in his office and whom McLaughlin knew from work together on a federal Drug Task Force, to meet with Fee to go over the records. McLaughlin arranged for Moran to meet with Fee, and Fee turned over all the documentation to him.

McLaughlin's testimony solved one of the mysteries in the case, as it had never been clear until then how the information on Wheel's false pay vouchers had found its way from the superior court in Burlington to the attorney general's office. "I thought there was something definitely wrong here, and that an investigation was needed," McLaughlin testified, noting that he pursued the allegations because "any alleged violation of law, whether it is federal, state, or whatever, I define within my duties."

Fee testified at the motions hearing that during the six month period between March and September 1985, Wheel filed for state pay for 139 days but only attended court hearings on 34 of those days. Ironically, he testified that he first started observing whether assistant judges were attending hearings after Wheel herself had expressed concern that her colleague, Charles Delaney, was not sitting on cases while putting in for pay. Fee found no issues with Delaney's records, but found the discrepancies in Wheel's pay vouchers. On cross-examination Fee acknowledged that he had a feeling of "vengeance" toward Wheel because she had stopped talking to him and was writing nasty letters about him to Justice Hill. "I was disturbed, angered and upset about the whole situation," he said. Fee also testified that in recent weeks he had been receiving anonymous threats in the mail, including a cartoon of a body being chopped up, with a picture of his head superimposed.

In a further effort to show that investigators had substantial evidence that led them to pursue the investigation, prosecutors called Moran to testify how he had reviewed close to 500 court files for the six-week period in April and May 1985. "We were looking for anything where Judge Wheel's name appeared in that period" to show whether she had been in court during this period, Moran testified, adding that he came up empty-handed. He cited the affidavits from two former deputy clerks stating that they were present at court hearings that Wheel did not attend and therefore they had not put her name on the file jackets, as would normally have been the case. Moran testified that "[t]hese particular file jackets had the name of Judge Wheel written down when it was not supposed to be there."

Wheel had claimed that signing notary certifications was part of what she had been doing on the days in question and had claimed pay for that work. Moran testified at the motions hearing that he asked the assistant judges in all fourteen counties whether they considered signing a notarial certification a function that made them eligible for compensation. The assistant judges all agreed that state pay could only be collected for sitting in the courtroom, signing court orders, or reading through the files, and that signing notarial certifications did not qualify them for state pay.

It would take Judge McCaffrey three months to consider all the arguments, but in July 1987 he finally issued a 60 page decision on all the pre-trial motions. He found "no evidence of misconduct or bias that would warrant disqualification of the attorney general's office or dismissal of the charges." He held that Judge Levitt had acted properly in not disqualifying herself from the case because of her earlier relationship with Suntag, noting that an attorney from Wing's law firm knew about the relationship and that they had agreed not to raise it as an issue. "As to the claim of judicial impropriety, this court determines that Judge Levitt at all times acted in an appropriate and responsible manner." Wing had also claimed that Levitt had showed prejudice toward Wheel by twice asking her not to interrupt Suntag during the inquest hearing. In rejecting this claim, McCaffrey pointed out that "Judge Levitt also admonished both the Defendant and Mr. Suntag during the May 13th inquest. We do not find this evidence of bias or prejudice."

McCaffrey found no merit in the argument that the attorney general inappropriately sent Hoff to see if Wheel would drop her re-election bid. To him, the evidence demonstrated that "[t]he attorney general never entered into any agreement with Sen. Hoff, nor was Sen. Hoff ever authorized to commit the attorney general to any matter under investigation." McCaffrey also dismissed the defense's claim that the new definition of assistant judges' official duties, which Justice Hill had orchestrated shortly after charges were brought against Wheel, applied retroactively to cover Wheel's alleged actions in this case.

The defense had also challenged the constitutionality of the inquest proceeding, and more than half of McCaffrey's opinion was devoted to the issue of whether the inquest procedure was constitutional. In another case decided a few months earlier, District Court Judge Frank Mahady had found the inquest proceeding violated the separation of powers doctrine by involving a judge (from the judiciary branch) in a criminal investigation by the attorney general's office (executive branch). In declaring the inquest proceeding unconstitutional, Mahady had written, "It is not for judges to collect and marshal evidence; that is the job of the prosecutor." While not binding on other courts, Mahady's decision gave McCaffrey great pause. He traced the doctrine of separation of powers back to Montesquieu, whose influence on James Madison was reflected in the Federalist papers. McCaffrey noted that neither Montesquieu nor Madison envisioned a complete separation of powers and that the doctrine as adopted in the nation's Constitution contemplated a system in which the branches of government must be connected and blended to some degree, with the permitted overlap also serving to help each branch keep watch over the other.

Focusing on the limited role played by a judge in an inquest proceeding, McCaffrey concluded that the mere administration of an oath of truthfulness and presence of a judge during questioning of witnesses did not serve to make the judiciary overly involved in the executive function. He held that "the judicial participation provided under Vermont inquest statutes does not violate the structure of government mandated by the Vermont Constitution. The division of powers need not be absolute; the amount of overlap here does not rise to an unconstitutional level."

McCaffrey also rejected Wheel's claim that she was deprived of the presence of counsel during the inquest in violation of the federal and Vermont constitutions, noting that, "Even had counsel been present, and even had the case under investigation gone to trial, counsel could have done nothing at the inquest by way of protecting the defendant's right of cross-examination, as there were no witnesses against defendant who could have been cross-examined." He pointed out that it was only after the inquest that Wheel faced criminal charges.

Wheel did get one small bit of good news from McCaffrey's decision on the motions. The stenographer who was present and transcribed the testimony at the May 13 inquest had not been duly sworn to secrecy as required by law and, in fact, had shared the notes with another stenographer, who helped her transcribe them. Prosecutors argued that even though the stenographer had not signed the form stating she had been sworn to secrecy, it was only a "technical" defect, as she was authorized to be at the secret proceeding. McCaffrey disagreed, noting that Vermont law strictly construes the requirement for secrecy at inquests. Since two of the six charges of perjury had come from that inquest hearing, McCaffrey dismissed those charges. He also combined two others charges, leaving Wheel facing trial on three charges of false swearing. It was a blow of sorts to the prosecution, but then again, Wheel's maximum sentence was reduced from 90 to 45 years in prison—hardly much for her to cheer over.

The parties reacted as expected. "Let's get on with the trial," Suntag responded, "This decision lets us go to trial, and that is exactly what we want to do." He added that he was not surprised at how long it had taken so far, "I don't think we've reached a year yet. That kind of delay in a case like this one I don't think is particularly unusual." Wing expressed disappointment with the decision, and when asked if this was the final roadblock to Wheel's criminal trial, said "I still suspect there will be some motions filed, but basically, the answer to your question is yes."

Wing did attempt to appeal Judge McCaffrey's denial of his pretrial motions, but the Supreme Court denied the request, writing that, even if there were errors in the conduct of the inquest, those errors would not offer a defense to the false swearing charge. "Accordingly," the Court wrote, "we cannot find that the issues defendant has raised are controlling or that their immediate resolution in this Court will materially advance the termination of the litigation." The denial of all defense motions meant that Wheel would be standing trial on the criminal charges.

## B. JUSTICES CHARGED WITH ETHICS VIOLATIONS

On January 28, 1987, following a five-month investigation, the Judicial Conduct Board formally charged Vermont Supreme Court Justices William Hill, Thomas Hayes and Ernest Gibson with violating the Code of Judicial Conduct on twenty-four different occasions in an attempt to protect Wheel from a criminal investigation and to intervene on her behalf in disputes between her and employees at the Chittenden courthouse. Judge Wheel herself was charged with six counts of misconduct. It marked the first time a Vermont Supreme Court justice was charged with violating the Code of Judicial Conduct.

The Code of Judicial Conduct establishes standards for the ethical conduct of judges. It contains broad statements called canons with specific rules set forth under each canon. Intrinsic to the entire Code is the expectation that judges must respect and honor the judicial office as a public trust and strive to enhance and maintain confidence in the state's legal system. Judicial conduct boards act as investigative agencies charged with evaluating complaints of code violations brought against judges. They are empowered to issue formal charges and hold evidentiary hearings, after which they may recommend to the Supreme Court that disciplinary action be taken. Possible disciplinary actions include public reprimand, suspension for a part or all of the remainder of a judge's term of office, or compelled retirement of a judge if physically or mentally disabled.

In Vermont the Supreme Court appoints the nine members of the Board, three of whom are lawyers, three are lay citizens, and three are judges. Over the years Vermont had had very few serious ethical issues in its judiciary, and what few there have been were initiated following a citizen complaint against a judge. In this case, however, the Judicial Conduct Board, based on what its members were reading in the local media, acted on its own initiative to bring ethical charges against the judges. It was an important act establishing the Board's role as proactive in protecting judicial integrity.

Justice Hill had no immediate comment to the charges. Justice Hayes, who was in treatment for his illness, emphatically denied the charges. In a prepared statement, he said, "I firmly believe that when the tumult and the shooting die, when all the evidence is in, and all the facts have been weighed, the Judicial Conduct Board will conclude that I have performed my duties as a judge fairly and impartially, free from any wrong or appearance of wrong." He pleaded with the public to withhold its judgment of him: "At a time when a complaint had been filed by the Judicial Conduct Board as a result of media reports, I believe that you will wait until all the evidence is in before you pass judgment on one who has served you all of his adult life."

Justice Gibson also released a statement denying that any of his actions were in any way influenced by reason of his acquaintance with Assistant Judge Wheel: "All actions taken by me as a justice of the Vermont Supreme Court that may be thought to be related in any way to the investigation of any charges against Judge Wheel have been motivated solely for the purpose of seeing that justice be administrated fairly and impartiality for the best interests of the people of the state of Vermont."

The ethics charges against three justices of the state's highest court sent profound shock waves through the legal community and throughout the state. The charges confirmed what many had feared the most: that these events would forever taint the reputation of the Court and the state's judicial system. Calling it a "sad day for the Vermont judiciary," Governor Kunin, who had appointed Hayes, said, "I hope that the process can be handled as quickly as possible and that we can set this dark cloud aside. It's a very difficult, painful situation." Peter Welch, president of the state Senate, noted the profound negative impact of the situation. "The Supreme Court is now operating under a cloud, and a very dark one at that. This is about the most unfortunate thing that could have happened," Welch said. Thomas Debvoise, a lawyer and former dean at Vermont Law

School, tried to minimize the impact, saying, "I don't think it's going to have any great long term effect on the judiciary at all. Out of it will come some guidelines to the high courts and its dealings with side judges."

The Conduct Board's complaint spanned a period of twelve years, and included several instances in which the justices had allegedly intervened on Wheel's behalf in matters at the Chittenden courthouse and had done so more recently to protect her from the attorney general's investigation. The highlights of the charges, published prominently in local newspapers, offered the public more details into some of the allegations being made by the justices. Twelve of the charges were leveled against Justice Hill. The first two alleged a relationship with Wheel that had long been rumored and which many had already assumed existed:

> *Count One:* In 1974 or 1975, when Justice Hill was on the Superior Court bench, the closeness of his friendship with Judge Wheel was so open that one employee of the Chittenden County Superior Court phoned Justice Hill at his home and warned him that unless he changed his way when he was in the presence of Judge Wheel, and unless Judge Wheel stopped her effusive praise of his intelligence, superior character and good looks, it would do serious damage to the reputation of them both.

> *Count Two:* In 1974 or 1975, when Justice Hill was on the Superior Court bench, Judge Wheel was in his chambers at the Chittenden Superior Court House. An employee of the Chittenden Superior Court walked into Justice Hill's chambers without knocking. She saw Judge Wheel standing behind Justice Hill, who was seated, and she saw Judge Wheel's arms around Justice Hill. Justice Hill became furious at the unannounced entry and he hollered at this employee and berated her for it such that she broke down and wept. Justice Hill saw this employee later in the day and he scolded her yet again.

The Board's complaint cited 10 instances of alleged misconduct by Justice Hayes, some of which had been previously reported, as well as others that were new. They included:

> *Count Six:* In February or March 1985, when Justice Hayes was on the Superior Court bench, he wrote and sent to Francis Fee, the Clerk of the Chittenden Superior Court,

a memo criticizing the operation of the Clerk's office and suggesting changes in its operation. Justice Hayes did so at the request of Judge Wheel and in order to please her, and he did so despite his own opinion that the criticism was unwarranted and the suggested changes unnecessary.

*Count Eight:* In March 1985 Justice Hayes attended a party honoring his elevation from the Superior Court to the Supreme Court. Among those in attendance was an employee of the Chittenden Superior Court whose competence in her job was beyond question. After the party was over, Justice Hayes made improper advances toward this employee, but she rebuffed him. On October 21, 1985, Justice Hayes attended a meeting with Justice Hill and Francis Fee. Mr. Fee, as Clerk of the Chittenden Superior Court, had the sole power to fire this employee. Justice Hill, with the tacit knowledge and consent of Justice Hayes, denigrated this employee and pressured Mr. Fee to discharge her from her job.

*Count Thirteen:* In November and December 1985, Senator Philip Hoff attempted to warn Justice Hayes that a principal cause of the problems at the Chittenden Superior Court was Judge Wheel's penchant for petty and vindictive actions. Senator Hoff further tried to warn Justice Hayes to sever his relationship with Judge Wheel in the interests of the judiciary and in the interests of maintaining his own reputation. Justice Hayes did not heed the warning, and continued his personal relationship with Judge Wheel. During the evening of November 26, 1985... Judge Wheel, from her home in Burlington, called Justice Hayes at the Brown Derby in Montpelier. They spoke to each other for 89 minutes. Judge Wheel charged the call to the Chittenden Superior Court. The length of the call, the closeness with which it followed notice of the attorney general's investigation, the time of day and the locus of the call combine to give the appearance of impropriety.

All three justices were charged with ethics violations for their role in organizing and sending the letter to Attorney General Amestoy expressing criticism over his handling of the Wheel investigation:

*Count Nineteen:* Sometime in May 1986, Justice Hill
invited Chief Justice Frederic W. Allen to his chambers.
Justices Hayes and Gibson were present at the arrival of
the Chief Justice. Justice Hill, with the apparent consent
and approval of Justice Hayes, suggested that Attorney
General Amestoy be summoned to appear before the
Supreme Court. Justice Hill, with the apparent consent
and approval of Justice Hayes, suggested that the Attorney
General's investigation of Judge Wheel might be politically motivated. Justice Hill, with the apparent consent
and approval of Justice Hayes, suggested that Mr. Amestoy
should be required to explain why the investigation was
taking so long. Justice Hill, with the apparent consent and
approval of Justice Hayes, also wanted to inquire of Mr.
Amestoy whether his office was responsible for leaks of
information to the press from secret inquests.

*Count Nineteen* went on to describe how Chief Justice Allen left Hill's
chambers and called a meeting of the full court "in one-half hour" and
then described what occurred there:

At this meeting, Justice Hayes moved that Mr. Amestoy
be summoned before the court for the purposes suggested
by Justice Hill earlier. Justice Hill seconded it. The motion
failed to carry, and Justice Hayes stormed out in anger.
Thereafter, Justice Hill, on behalf of the entire court,
signed and delivered a letter to Attorney General Amestoy
expressing the court's concern over the length of the investigation of Judge Wheel and over the inquest leaks.

Justice Gibson had never sat in the Chittenden court with Wheel
when he was on the superior court bench, and unlike Hill and Hayes, he
did not have a social relationship with Wheel. As a result, it was generally thought that his involvement with her was considerably less than the
other justices. The release of the charges bore that out. Gibson was named
in only seven of the misconduct counts, and his attorney, who described
Gibson's relationship with Wheel as "more of an acquaintanceship than
a social friendship," said that the allegations against Gibson would be
improper only if he had had a close relationship with Wheel.

The filing of ethics charges created an immediate problem for Justices
Hill and Gibson. Three weeks earlier they had participated in a hearing in

the Hunt case despite a defense request that they recuse themselves. Hunt's appellate attorney, Bill Nelson, who had been abused by Justice Hill the last time he had appeared before the Court, had specifically requested that Hill, Hayes, and Gibson disqualify themselves from "the decision on this motion and from any further participation in the Hunt appeal." Nelson pointed out that all three justices were "long-time personal friends of Judge Wheel" and added, "These facts alone make their further participation in the case at least arguably improper."

It did not deter Justices Hill and Gibson, who decided to participate in oral arguments on the motion. However, after the arguments the Court had taken the motion under advisement, and had not yet ruled on it when the ethics charges against the justices were filed. The filing of the ethics charges disqualified the justices from continuing to participate in the Hunt case. Shortly after the ethical charges were released, Justices Hill and Gibson issued an extraordinary decision in which they first pointed out that Nelson's request that they recuse themselves from the Hunt hearing had been "based primarily on 'published reports' in the media." The justices cited cases from around the country which "with near uniformity have rejected unsupported opinion, baseless conclusions, rumors, gossip and hearsay as a proper basis for a recusal motion." Citing a federal circuit court decision, Hill and Gibson argued:

> Although public confidence may be as much shaken by publicized inferences of bias that are false as by those that are true, a judge considering whether to disqualify himself must ignore rumors, innuendos, erroneous information published as fact in newspapers… To find otherwise would allow an irresponsible, vindictive or self-interested press informant and/or an irresponsible, misinformed or careless reporter to control the choice of judge.[33]

Hill and Gibson went on to argue that if only newspaper reports were being considered, "we would violate our ethical duty and oath of office by recusing ourselves." However, the justices acknowledged that since disciplinary charges had been filed against them relating to a case then pending before them, recusal was required. Hill and Gibson made clear,

---

33    *State v. Hunt*, 147 Vt. 631 (1987)

however, that "there is no doubt in our minds that we could fairly and impartially decide the legal issues" in the Hunt appeal.[34]

The following year, the Hunt appeal would be finally argued on its merits at the Supreme Court. This time it was not quite a "rump" court, as Justice Louis Peck, one of the five sitting justices, sat on the appeal. The other justices had all disqualified themselves. Three superior court judges, Edward Costello, Silvio Valente and David Jenkins, along with retired Justice Barney, joined Peck on the bench to hear the appeal. Hunt would argue that the Supreme Court had no authority to transfer his case to Lamoille County and in doing so had prejudiced him at trial and violated his rights. The Court would ultimately reject his appeal, citing in a tortured opinion its duty to supervise the courts and declaring its responsibility "to provide a new slate of judges untainted by the unusual series of events which had taken place in this case prior to that time." Justice Peck, writing for the majority, noted that "[a]lthough in hindsight it might have been preferable for this Court to have dealt with this situation in another way, this Court's order moving the Hunt case to Lamoille County was reasonable, not draconian, and consistent with the high purposes of the judicial system."[35] This explanation was itself an attempt to justify an unprecedented and inexcusable decision by the Court to protect Jane Wheel.

Only Acting Justice Silvio Valente had the courage to dissent from this extraordinary decision. He noted, correctly, that the issue presented was "whether the Supreme Court may, on its own motion, assume jurisdiction of a matter not pending before it without providing notice and an opportunity to be heard by the litigants." Finding no authority anywhere supporting such action, Valente argued that, notwithstanding the Supreme Court's supervisory role, it lacked jurisdiction in the case, so that its order changing the venue of the case to Lamoille County was void. In the end Gordon Hunt would spend 20 years in jail. He was released in 2005.

On Monday, February 2, 1987, five days after release of the charges against the justices and Wheel, Wheel's term as an assistant judge came to an end. While a collective sigh of relief could be felt throughout the legal community, it was especially loud at the Burlington courthouse, where employees had suffered through years of tension and discord. They had been waiting months for a pay raise and had formed a union the previous year to seek protection and a mechanism to raise their voices

---

34  Id.
35  *State v. Hunt*, 150 Vt. 483 (1988)

against her authoritarian rule. The newly elected assistant judge, Elizabeth Gretkowski, said she was not concerned that the employees at the courthouse had formed a union. "I think it's too bad it had to come to this," she said, "but due to past working conditions it had to." Both Gretkowski and Delaney, who was elected to his second term, indicated that they would meet with the employees and settle the wage dispute. It was clear Wheel would not be missed around the courthouse.

With her tenure as an assistant judge over, and her criminal trial bogged down in pretrial motions and discovery, Wheel turned her attention to the Board's allegations of misconduct against her. She had been charged with six counts of misconduct, which included an alleged intimate relationship with Hill and a charge of "haughtiness and disrespect" with which she had treated the employees at the Chittenden courthouse. Her attorney, Leonard Wing, came out swinging, arguing that the ethics charges were "full of untruths and mistaken facts, and was filed for the purposes of harassment." He filed several motions attacking Board members and challenging the allegations in the complaint. As Wheel had lost the election and was no longer a judge, Wing also argued the Board had no jurisdiction over her and should dismiss the complaint. He also moved to disqualify all seven members of the Board, claiming that its chairman, Richard Mallary, had made public comments earlier in the investigation which indicated the Board members had made up their minds before the conclusion of the investigation.

In a separate argument, Wing asked the Board to disqualify Board member Fred Parker, arguing that a lawyer in Parker's law firm had filed briefs in the Hunt case opposing the authority of assistant judges to reject plea agreements, and that another member of Parker's law firm had assisted courthouse employees in forming a union to protect themselves from Wheel. "Both of these attorneys have represented parties in direct conflict with Judge Wheel's position in the recent past," Wing wrote, adding "Under these circumstances, Mr. Parker's impartiality may reasonably be questioned and he must be disqualified from sitting on the board."

Hayes was still in a Boston hospital undergoing treatment for lung cancer, but his lawyer, Richard Davis, joined Wing in moving to disqualify members of the Board based on Mallary's statements. Davis argued that "[t]he pettiness of these meritless charges, the havoc this proceeding is causing in the judicial system, as well as the emotional distress inflicted upon Justice Hayes and others—all these considerations compel the swift termination of these accusations." Davis was also highly critical of the Board for not informing the justices of the full nature of the allegations against them until they were served with the complaint. "With all due respect to the Board," Davis wrote, "this premeditated denial of Justice Hayes' right to respond to allegations prior to publication of the complaint conjures up images of the Spanish Inquisition and the Salem Witch Trials."

All three of the justices had been interviewed by prosecutors for the Board before the charges had been brought. None of the justices' statements had been released, but Davis decided to give a transcript of Hayes's interview with the prosecutors to a reporter covering the case. Hayes' statement to the Board's prosecutors sheds more light on some of the problems at the Chittenden courthouse over the previous few years and indicated how he had found himself caught up in them. He acknowledged receiving telephone calls from Wheel around the time she was summoned to appear at an inquest hearing, but he said he did not in any way direct her as to what to say. He included this pertinent observation, "I know my attorney would tell me not to volunteer anything, but I would like to put on the record a characterization of Judge Wheel so that these telephone calls can be put in perspective. Judge Wheel is a very aggressive woman, and if anybody does her a slight or renders her an indignation, she doesn't hesitate to call all of her friends who have a listening ear to recite the details of the slight. And many of the phone calls were based on indignations she suffered after she came under scrutiny."

During the interview, Board prosecutors had asked Hayes about rumors "that certain members of the Supreme Court have been intimate with Judge Wheel." Hayes responded, "Absolutely not, and it just came to my attention that there was a rumor about me...and I'm willing to take the oath with respect to that, the press saying I've been to bed with Judge Wheel," adding, "Nor do I have any basis that Justice Hill or Justice Gibson is having sexual relations or ever had. I heard a rumor 11 years ago about Justice Hill, and that's all it turned out to be." Hayes concluded the interview by charging that the press had overblown the story, saying, "I've been in Vermont public life since 1951, and I cannot recall anything from the Manson murders to the Hamlin slaying" (two young boys from Essex had seized two pre-teen girls on their way home from school, raped and stabbed them, killing one) to the impeachment of the president in which there have been so many stories of one event."

Hayes' statement offered some insights into how he came to be caught up in this scandal. He was a highly respected jurist and lawyer and a gentleman. A man of literature, he was known to read beautiful poetry when he officiated at the marriages of his friends. He served at a time when a conservative U.S. Supreme Court was limiting individual rights and privacy. He became a champion of the Vermont constitution, challenging the legal community to look there to "protect the rights and liberties of our people, however the philosophy of the United States Supreme Court may ebb and flow."[36]

Although he had a sharp legal mind, Hayes was ultimately a politician, and as a judge in the Chittenden court, he found himself caught up in Wheel's intrigues and political maneuverings. "Hayes wasn't able to separate politics from the job," one local lawyer said. "He came from a political background, where you were protected by your friends. Unfortunately, I think the system and the individuals came together at the wrong time." Another lawyer who knew Hayes suggested that he was particularly vulnerable to Wheel, noting that during Hayes tenure in the Chittenden court, he and Wheel would "talk, and talk and talk." He went on:

> What do you talk about when you talk, and talk and talk?
> You talk about personal things, about how your wife and
> children are doing. About how your friends and enemies
> are doing. You tell about the indiscretions in your life, and
> anything else like that, your aberrations and your failures.
> Sooner or later you become in the power of that person if
> that person is of the type to use it against you.[37]

Although Judge Morse understood Wheel was that kind of person, Judge Hayes obviously did not. Another lawyer acknowledged that many people were searching for the "missing piece," and suggested the answer could be simple: "She flattered him, same with Hill, gave him adulation," he said, "Politicians have fragile egos. Tom's a politician."

There was, however, another side to Hayes. Peter Freyne, who wrote a colorful column in the *Vermont Vanguard*, a weekly paper filled with political and other intrigues, had a way of giving appropriate nicknames to the political characters about whom he was writing. He had dubbed Wheel "Sweet Lady Jane," and Hayes was known in his column as "The Swordsman." Referring to Count Eight in the complaint, in which Hayes is accused of making advances on one of the court employees at a party,

---

36   *Vermont v. Jewett*, 500 A.2d 233 (1985)

37   *Burlington Free Press*, February 1, 1987

Freyne wrote, "We are left to guess just what kind of improper advances Hayes made. After all, Tom Hayes is known in judicial circles as 'The Swordsman,' a nickname he didn't get by service on the US Fencing team. For the sake of giving inquiring flatlanders something to shake their heads over," Freyne added, "let's suggest that the judge, in a low voice, suggested to the woman that they go somewhere and imitate Adam and Eve." [38]

Hayes' diagnosis of lung cancer had forced him to leave the bench for treatment, and on May 3, 1987, just three months after the Conduct Board charges were filed, Justice Hayes died. He was 60 years old. In a eulogy at his funeral, Chief Justice Allen said, "The State of Vermont has lost a truly eminent jurist. He was firmly dedicated to the principles contained in the Bill of Rights and Declaration of Rights and the constitutions of our nation and state." The Judicial Conduct Board would eventually dismiss the charges against Hayes.

It may be that some of Hayes' friends got it right. He had what he himself described as a "listening ear," and Wheel had seized on this kind and compassionate man, making him a "confidant" in all the personal schemes and intrigues in which she was engaged in the courthouse. And as the internal intrigues grew into investigations and inquests and criminal charges, Hayes remained that 'listening ear" long after he should have known better.

In responding to the justices' denials of the allegations of misconduct, the Board's prosecutors, William Donahue and Douglas Richards, maintained that the three Supreme Court justices had been caught up in Wheel's "thrall" and had engaged in a "byzantine effort" to protect her and keep her "content" at the expense of their other duties. They argued strongly that Vermonters had a right to "get to the bottom" of the relationship between Wheel and the three justices and that only a full public hearing of the "sordid affair" would restore confidence in the judiciary.

Justice Gibson had filed a motion asking the Board to sever his case from those of the other justices. He noted that he had never had a personal or social relationship with Wheel, and argued that he was charged in only a few of the counts, and did not want to be prejudiced by the charges against the other jurists. The Board's prosecutors opposed the motion, arguing that all the allegations were related to one another, and that Gibson's motion to sever was based on the distrust of the Board's ability to "separate out the evidence as it related to him from the evidence as it relates to the others." That fear, it was argued, was outweighed by the "heavy presumption" that the Board would discharge its duty fairly and without prejudice. The Board's prosecutors took particular issue with the justices' claim that the entire complaint should be dismissed because the allegations, even if true, failed to show any wrongdoing or misconduct. Finding that argument "most disturbing," the Board prosecutors argued that it showed the justices' "insensitivity to the ethical standards they are expected to follow."

In opposing the justices' motion to disqualify the entire Conduct Board, Board prosecutors wrote, "To bow to the request for disqualification...would be to capitulate to their unjudicial tantrum." Board prosecutors asserted that the motions were intended as a "tactic" to avoid the charges and added that the 'best defense is a good offense' is a "...tactic that does not become the legal profession. They must be called to account if public confidence in our judicial system is to be restored."

Wing himself was asking the Board to dismiss the ethics charges against Wheel, and one of his arguments caught the attention of the Board. Pointing out that the Board rules did not authorize discipline of retired judges, Wing asked the Board to dismiss the misconduct charges against Wheel because she no longer sat on the bench. He argued that the cloud that had hung over the judiciary lifted with Wheel's failed re-election bid and that to continue to pursue the case against her would "create a new storm of controversy" that would go against the public interest. He also noted that the most serious penalty the Board could impose would be removal from the bench, which was now no longer an option. Board prosecutors vigorously opposed the motion, arguing that the Board retained the right to discipline Wheel even though she was no longer on the bench. They argued that the public interest would be served by having the Board "get to the bottom" of the allegations and determine whether there was wrongdoing and a need to reform the court system; the Board could issue a reprimand to Wheel or prevent her from running again for public office.

The Board was clearly concerned about this issue. After hearing arguments from both sides, it decided to ask the Supreme Court to determine whether the Board had the power to sanction a former judge. In its petition to the Court, the Board noted that it "is not structured to issue rulings on questions of law such as are raised by Judge Wheel's motion to dismiss." The Board noted that "substantial public and private resources may be expended fruitlessly should it later be determined that the Board did not have jurisdiction with regard to the formal complaint against Judge Wheel," a result that "could undermine public confidence in the judicial process."

The Board also brought to the Supreme Court's attention that Justice Hill had elected to retire from the bench a few months earlier rather than face a retention hearing in the legislature.[39] Although Hill had not filed a motion asking that charges against him be dismissed, the Conduct Board made the Court aware that its decision regarding the Board's authority to discipline retired judges would also impact its authority in the Hill case. The recommendation from the Board to ask the Supreme Court to decide the issue was signed by all of the Conduct Board members. Wheel's attorney was only too happy to have the Supreme Court decide the issue. "I have absolutely no objection whatsoever because I feel it would end up there anyway," Wing said, adding that if the Board had decided to go forward on the case, he would have tried to appeal the issue himself. Hill's attorney, Michael Marks, agreed that the Board's request made sense, as "[w]ithout a forum to vindicate him, there will always be a cloud, but on the other hand, if the Court rules the Judicial Conduct Board no longer has jurisdiction on Justice Hill, at least it would put an end to this unfortunate chapter."

The fact that the Board had taken the unusual step of asking the Supreme Court to clarify whether it had the authority to recommend discipline of a former judge was an indication of how uncertain, and how important, the answer was to the question. Since neither Hill nor Wheel were judges at this point, the decision would determine whether they would face trial on the misconduct charges or whether all the ethics charges would simply be dismissed. As the hearing approached, local media let it be known its feelings on the matter. Calling the Hill and Wheel allegations a "stain" on the judiciary, an editorial in the *Burlington Free Press* opined that dismissing the charges against the judges would "drastically damage the ability of the court system to police itself. In the future, no judge would have to fear being disciplined for unethical conduct. He or she could avoid accountability by simply stepping down from the bench."[40]

In their brief to the Court on the issue, Board prosecutors noted the seriousness of the case at hand: "Today time has brought over our

---

39   Judges appointed by the Governor undergo a retention hearing in the legislature every six years.

40   Editorial, *Burlington Free Press,* August 15, 1987

judiciary a troubling pall. The framers of our constitution could not fore-
tell this event. If our constitution is to remain vital," they added, "it must
be interpreted in such a way that the pall is lifted." Citing a plethora of
cases from other jurisdictions supporting their argument, the prosecuting
lawyers urged the Court to accept disciplinary responsibility for former
judges and "dispel the cloud that hangs over our judiciary. The integrity
of the judicial process will not be preserved and public confidence in the
judiciary will not be maintained here by holding that this court lacks
jurisdiction over Wheel and Hill."

It didn't take the Supreme Court long to decide the issue. On July
23, 1987, less than two weeks after oral arguments, the Court issued a
one-page order holding that the Judicial Conduct Board had authority to
recommend discipline of former judges. The Court noted the absence of
any statute or constitutional provision exempting former judicial officers
from discipline and then, rejecting the *Fienberg* case as precedent, held
that, "It is the view of this court that jurisdiction for purposes of judicial
discipline attaches when a complaint is filed during judicial tenure relating
to acts done as a judicial officer..."[41] Board prosecutors were pleased, but
not surprised, by the ruling. "I expected that the Supreme Court would
rule this way because all of the precedents indicated that they would have
to," Donahue said, adding that the ruling "means that all the facts will
come out in a public forum and I'm confident justice will be done."

Justice Hayes had died a few months earlier, and charges against
him had been dismissed. Charges against Justice Gibson, which had
always been viewed as the least serious, were also dropped after he publicly acknowledged that some of his actions had created an appearance
of impropriety and that he could have acted differently in some of the
circumstances concerning Wheel. This left only Hill and Wheel to face
trial on the ethics charges before the Board.

While the Conduct Board had the motions and arguments under advisement, Board prosecutors filed new misconduct charges against Hill. In doing
so, they filled in some gaps on what had been known publicly to that point.
The new charges alleged that while Justice Hill and Wheel were socializing
together at the Holiday Inn in Burlington, Hill had told Wheel that Morse,
the presiding judge, did not have the authority to disqualify her from participating in the Hunt case. Board prosecutors alleged that Hill suggested to
Wheel that she appeal Morse's decision and that he would change the venue

---

41  *In re Hill*, 152 Vt. 575 (1987)

in the case, thereby avoiding the embarrassment the disqualification had caused her. The new charges asserted that these conversations violated Hill's ethical obligations and that he should not have participated in later Supreme Court deliberations when these issues later came before the Court.

Hill's lawyers, Carl Lisman and Michael Marks, vigorously objected to the new charges. They pointed out that Hill had not been advised of the charges in advance, as required by the rules, and thus they urged the Board to reject them. Had Board prosecutors "spoken with Justice Hill to have determined the true facts of the matter, his innocence would have been established and these charges could have been avoided," they argued. The Conduct Board took the motion under advisement.

There were a few minor skirmishes between the lawyers in the waning months of the year, but as 1988 was about to start, everything appeared finally on track to begin both the Hill ethics trial before the Judicial Conduct Board and Wheel's criminal trial in Rutland District Court. Justice Hill had been waiting more than a year for a trial on his misconduct charges and, with all the preliminary issues finally resolved, his attorneys advised the Board that he was ready to go to trial. Hill asked the Board to sever his case from Wheel's, arguing that they were charged together in only three of the allegations and that the "overlap is far too little to justify continuing a joint proceeding." Wheel's attorneys did not object to having Hill tried separately. They argued that it would confuse the Board to have to "sift through" the evidence to determine which facts applied to which judge. Wing also noted that Hill was interested in an expedited trial, while Wheel was interested in delaying her misconduct trial until her criminal trial was resolved. Board prosecutors opposed the request to separate the trials, arguing that trying the two cases together would provide "more convenience and economy. If tried separately, or together," as "the same issues will come up."

The Board acted quickly, issuing a decision within two days ordering that Hill and Wheel be tried separately. The ruling held both good news and bad news for Hill. While it separated his case from Wheel's, the Board also granted the state's request to add the additional misconduct counts against Hill, charging him with inappropriately discussing the Hunt murder case with Wheel and failing to recuse himself when issues involving the Hunt case had come before the Supreme Court. Shortly after the Court's ruling severing the two cases, Wing asked McCaffrey for permission to withdraw as Wheel's attorney in the criminal case, as he would likely testify as a witness about what had occurred at the inquest. After a brief hearing, McCaffrey granted the motion, and Richard Davis, a well-known and respected criminal defense attorney who had previously represented Hayes in the ethics case before the Board, entered an appearance on Wheel's behalf. McCaffrey advised the lawyers that the criminal trial would begin in January and that he was setting aside four weeks to try the case.

As Hill's misconduct trial approached, Davis advised Board prosecutors, as well as the attorney general that, although Wheel wanted to testify in Hill's misconduct trial, it could hurt her defense in her criminal trial. He also told them it would force her to choose between testifying at the Hill hearing or asserting her right under the Fifth Amendment not to incriminate herself. For perhaps the first time in this long, evolving saga, there was agreement among Wheel's attorney, the Board prosecutors, and the attorney general. In early January 1988, they joined in a petition asking the Board to postpone Hill's misconduct trial until after the conclusion of Wheel's criminal trial. Attorney General Amestoy told the Board that holding Hill's misconduct trial first would reveal legal theories and strategies that might be used against Wheel during her criminal trial and also might force her to invoke her Fifth Amendment rights. Either way, he argued, Wheel would be faced with adverse publicity. Hill's attorneys vigorously objected to any postponement of his misconduct trial. They argued the delay would "cause severe harm to Justice Hill" and pointed out that Hill's children had made arrangements to be with him at the hearing, that he had incurred legal debts totaling more than $5,000 preparing for the hearing, and that he had a constitutional right to a prompt hearing. They argued that Hill should not have to suffer the additional strain of "looking forward to trial and then perhaps having it snatched away."

The Board had denied the request, and all three parties appealed the denial to the Supreme Court. The attorney general cited "several dangers" that could arise if the Hill hearing were held prior to Wheel's criminal trial, noting that each of the counts of misconduct against Hill explicitly mentioned Wheel. Davis pointed out that "once testimony is taken in Hill's case, there is the distinct possibility that we will then be confronted with media publicity where witnesses will be quoted." He also noted that if Wheel were called as a witness in the conduct case and refused to testify on the grounds of self-incrimination, it could also prejudice her in front of a jury in her criminal case. Board prosecutors joined in the request, noting that "Judge Wheel's testimony is important in the Judicial Conduct

Board's proceeding against Justice Hill because the nature and extent of her relationship with Justice Hill lies at the heart of the case."

Amestoy would later describe the conference the parties had in Justice Barney's chambers before argument on the case. With all the parties present, Barney passed a note over to the court reporter. The note said, "Turn off the tape recorder." Barney then explained that he wanted the parties to know that there had almost been a "Saturday night massacre." He went on to say that an unsuccessful effort had been made to reconstitute the "rump" court that was going to decide whether Hill's case would go forward or be delayed. He did not elaborate further, and although the implication was that a newly configured Court would be sympathetic to letting the Hill case go forward without delay, everyone was left to wonder about the Saturday night massacre that almost was.

The high Court issued its ruling the following day, three days before Hill's trial was scheduled to begin. The Court took particular note that Judge McCaffrey had stated that if Wheel were required to testify at Hill's ethics trial, her rights in the criminal case pending before him would be impaired to the point that she probably would be denied a fair trial. "In view of the conclusions of Judge McCaffrey, and the assertions of counsel for Jane Wheel," the Court wrote, "we direct the Board to continue the final hearing in the Hill case until after the conclusion of the trial in *State v. Wheel*."[42] The Court was, however, not unsympathetic to Hill's position. Finding that the attorney general's office did not bring forward the concern with sufficient diligence to minimize the harm to Hill, the Court authorized the Board to order the attorney general's office to pay for additional legal costs suffered by Hill as a result of having his case delayed.

---

42   *Hill and State of Vermont v. Wheel*, 149 Vt. 203 (January 15, 1988).

# PART THREE

*The Trials*

## A. WHEEL GOES TO TRIAL

On Monday, January 25, 1988, more than two years after allegations of "improprieties" first appeared as headlines in newspapers across the state, former Assistant Judge Jane Wheel finally appeared in Rutland District Court to face three felony counts of lying under oath. Wheel arrived at the courthouse alone, with no family or friends present. She took her seat between her two lawyers, appearing nervous as she leaned over to consult with them.

During questioning of potential jurors, Wheel's attorney, Richard Davis, repeatedly asked if they understood that some questions can be posed in a way to elicit two different answers. "A witness might misunderstand a question and answer erroneously," Davis said, "We're going to be dealing with some very precise questions." Suntag asked jurors to concentrate on the four basic elements of the charges presented by the State: that Wheel took an oath at the 1986 inquest, that she lied, that she did so willfully, and that she lied about a subject for which she took the oath. "If you keep your focus on these four essential elements," Suntag, said, "which is your duty throughout the trial, you'll do fine."

Judge McCaffrey advised the potential jurors that he had not yet decided if the jury would be sequestered in a hotel at the end of each day for the duration of the trial, which was projected to last at least two weeks. As the jurors waited to be questioned by the attorneys, they joked nervously about the prospect of spending weeks together in seclusion. One prospective juror was observed sobbing quietly. It would take three full days of questioning more than one hundred Rutland County residents before the lawyers finally agreed on the ten women and two men who would decide Wheel's fate. Two female jurors were chosen as alternates. Just minutes after the jury was finally seated, McCaffrey told them what many had feared—that because of the publicity surrounding the trial, they would be separated from their families and sequestered in a local hotel for the duration of the trial. In making his ruling, the judge told the jurors, "In fairness to both sides, it's critical you not be tainted in any way," adding they should not discuss the case even among themselves.

The long-awaited trial finally began on Friday morning, January 29, 1988. Davis used his opening statement to describe Wheel as a "loyal and dedicated" assistant judge who attended court virtually every day, had nothing to cover up, and had no reason to lie under oath. Addressing the jury for 45 minutes without notes, Davis first described the tension between Wheel and the court clerk, Frank Fee. He said he would show that Wheel was the target of a vendetta by Fee, who was fearful of losing his job, and he charged that Fee had a friend initiate the attorney general's investigation that Wheel was being paid for days she did not work. Davis also told the jury that the legislature had written vaguely worded statutes on how assistant judges were to be paid, and that the Burlington courthouse suffered from poor bookkeeping, causing confusion about who signed file jackets. He described how the charges had turned Wheel's life into a nightmare, forcing her out of office and costing her most of her friends. "She's virtually been a hermit," he told the jury. "She even has to go to the grocery store in the middle of the night."

The state's first witness was Diane Lavallee, the deputy clerk in the Burlington court. Lavallee portrayed Wheel as a bully who threatened to fire court employees. "You just didn't question Judge Wheel," she testified. "She told me she had the power to fire anyone and she would do it to the first person who got her name in the paper." Lavallee described how Wheel claimed to have worked 30 days in March 1985, but that she had not sat in court a single day that month because she was planning a party for Judge Hayes. In his cross-examination, Davis fired questions at Lavallee about conversations, dates, and motivations, and he became more and more frustrated by Lavallee's vague recollections. The tension between the two erupted as Davis pressed Lavallee as to why she had testified at the 1986 inquest probe. "The reason you did that was because you don't like her," Davis said. "I don't respect her," Lavallee responded, tilting her head and body away from Davis, as she did throughout most of his questioning. "You don't like her," Davis said again. "I guess not," Lavallee conceded.

Lavallee testified that Wheel stopped talking to Fee in April, 1985, because, "He had gone to lunch with Justice Wynn Underwood, and she didn't want him to do this." She added that she became the go-between for Fee and Wheel until Wheel stopped talking to her as well. Lavallee was familiar with the handwriting of several different court employees and pointed out to the jury where she believed Wheel had added her name to the jacket covers. The jury then got its first look at the file jackets, passing them around and examining them for nearly 20 minutes.

Lavallee was finally dismissed after three long, tedious days on the witness stand, and the state called Randall Moran as its next witness. Moran, who had been a criminal investigator for nine years, told the jury that he had reviewed approximately 350 case files covering a six-week period from

March 5 through April 12, 1986, to see if Wheel's name was on any of those files. Moran also described his numerous interviews with clerks, stenographers, and judges for their recollections of Wheel's presence during that period. When asked if his research had found any evidence indicating Wheel had sat on any cases during that period, Moran's reply was a short "No, sir."

Moran described how he took another look at the file jackets after learning that Wheel had gone back to the courthouse to "correct" the records, and he found that Wheel's name had been added to several of the file jackets. He also testified that he found her name on one court order inside a file, with her signature written over a squiggle mark that the presiding judge had drawn in the blank space beneath his own signature. Moran told the jury that he had looked at the copies of the order that had been sent to the lawyers, and those copies did not have Wheel's name on them. He had spoken with Judge David Jenkins, who had put the squiggle mark in the blank space under his name, and Jenkins had confirmed to him that he had placed a squiggle line through the block for assistant judges' names because no assistant judges were present to sign the order.

Davis' cross-examination of Moran went on literally for days and was relentless. He led Moran through paper trails and computer records of dates the state claimed Wheel had improperly altered the files. Davis attacked Moran for never interviewing Wheel herself. "She could have been reviewing cases, signing orders, signing notaries, things of that sort," Davis said. Moran responded that the prosecution made a decision not to interview Wheel. At one point, Davis had Moran identify three file jackets on which the signature alleged to be that of Judge Wheel differed from her ordinary and usual method of writing a "W" and "h." As a result, Wheel would not have been lying, Davis argued, when she answered, "I don't write like that," to one of the inquest questions. Moran responded by telling the jurors that the state would be calling a handwriting expert to testify in the case. Davis again attacked Moran for not bothering to check whether Wheel had performed other official duties, such as discussing court facilities with presiding judges, which Davis argued would have entitled Wheel to receive state pay. Moran conceded that there were duties other than sitting on cases in court that could make an assistant judge eligible for state pay, but he added that "[p]lanning parties would not be the type of thing that a judge should get paid for."

After five days with Moran on the witness stand undergoing repetitive cross-examination, Suntag had had enough, saying "We would object to the needless repetition. He's had ample opportunity to explore this area for days and days." Citing the Rules of Evidence, Suntag argued that the court should exercise "reasonable control so as to avoid needless consumption of time and…protect witnesses from harassment." As the weary jury looked on, McCaffrey politely denied Suntag's request. Moran finally stepped down after six days on the witness stand. He had remained calm and courteous throughout the long, drawn-out cross-examination, and to the end, he maintained that none of the criticism of his work had changed his findings or his opinion that Wheel had lied under oath. It was an emotionally charged case, and it was spilling out in the length and detail of the questioning, and the aggressive manner of both sides. The firestorm of controversy that had engulfed Wheel and three members of the Vermont Supreme Court was described by the local press as having "wounded the integrity of the Vermont judiciary."

The heart of the state's case was whether Wheel lied when she denied that signatures on some file folders were hers. Edward Smith, a handwriting analyst with the U.S. Postal Service, told the jury that the signatures on a number of case file folders were Jane Wheel's signatures. Using an enlargement showing the disputed signatures next to Wheel's known signature, Smith described how he compared the signatures on the folders to the samples Wheel had been ordered to give to the attorney general's office: "If we look at the some of the characteristics I observed, we can see a pattern in all the names on the file folders that matches the samples" that Wheel gave to the state. When asked if it was his opinion that the signatures could not have been made by anyone but Wheel, Smith answered, "Correct."

As Davis began his cross-examination of Smith, the defense shifted tactics. Davis now conceded that Wheel had in fact signed all but one of the file folders, the one that had an unusual, stick-like "W." Davis showed Smith a stack of notary certificates signed by Wheel and said, "I'll ask you to point out a single occasion where the 'W' is written as it is in the court file she denies recognizing as hers." Smith said he could find no other instance in which Wheel had signed her name that way. "Isn't it true that when Wheel said, 'No, I don't write like that,' that was a correct statement?" Smith reply: "No sir." Davis pressed harder, "She normally starts with a loop through the 'W'?" Smith replied, "She makes two types of 'W's," and added that although rare, the signature was nonetheless Wheel's.

Lee Suskin followed Smith to the witness stand and described to the jury how he had interviewed Wheel for three hours in February 1986, as part of a study he was performing on how to improve operations at the Chittenden courthouse. Reading from notes he took during the interview, Suskin testified that Wheel had told him that the court records were in a "sad state" and that "she and her husband had worked Saturdays to correct the jacket entries." It was this information that had prompted the attorney general's office to go back to the courthouse to review the file folders and to discover that Wheel's signature had been added to the folders. Suskin also described a meeting two months later with Wheel and Charles Delaney, the other assistant judge. Wheel became angry at Suskin because he had failed to criticize Fee adequately. "Judge Wheel was upset with me for constantly referring to the Clerk's cooperation and not telling Judge Delaney what a bad job Frank was doing as clerk," Suskin said, adding that when Delaney left the room, Wheel "raised her voice and started screaming at me."

In a case already filled with "firsts," the state called Chief Justice Allen to the witness stand, making him the first sitting chief justice to testify at a criminal trial. Allen filled in a hole in the timeline in the state's case. One of the file folders with Wheel's name on it had been sent from the Burlington court to the Supreme Court on November 30, 1985. Davis argued that by the time Wheel found out about the investigation in late December, this file folder was already at the Supreme Court, making it impossible for her to have added her signature to it. Allen told the jury that in November, approximately a month before the investigation became public, he told Wheel that the attorney general's office had requested her pay vouchers and asked her if she wanted to claim that the pay vouchers were privileged. Allen testified that he and Wheel had three telephone conferences about the issue, and she had agreed to release the documents. This was important testimony, as it showed that the file folder in question was, in fact, still at the Burlington courthouse when Wheel learned she was under investigation.

McCaffrey announced to the jury that an afternoon court session would be delayed to allow him time to meet with the attorneys in the case. The judge made no more explicit explanation for the delay but after a four hour delay, he advised the jury that one of the female jurors had been excused from the jury panel, and he instructed one of the two alternate jurors to take the vacant seat. It would later be reported that the juror was excused after experiencing distress at being apart from her family for so long.

The state's last witness was Judge Mathew Katz, who told the jury that while he and Wheel were sitting on a divorce case, Wheel had signed both their names on the case file folder and said to him, "You know,

Mathew, if we don't watch out for these things, we don't get credit for them." His testimony was important to counter Wheel's sworn testimony at the inquest that she never wrote on a file jacket. As Katz left the witness stand on February 13th, and after more than two weeks of testimony from thirteen witnesses, the prosecution finally rested its perjury case against Jane Wheel.

As the trial moved into its third week, Wheel began her defense by calling her former attorney, Leonard Wing, as her first witness. Wing told the jury that when news of the pay voucher investigation first became public, he had advised Wheel to go to the courthouse on a Saturday to look at the files to see if it was true that her name did not appear on any case files during the six-week period in question. He testified that he "cautioned her to make sure that all she did is go through those files," and told the jury he told Wheel not to correct any file she thought contained errors, but instead to "take it out and show it to the clerk." Wing also previewed for the jury Wheel's new explanation for having said under oath that she never wrote in a file folder. He told the jury that when Wheel stated at the inquest that she never signed her name to court files, she understood she was responding only to the Saturday she had gone to the courthouse with her husband. "Jane Wheel felt that this particular testimony dealt with the one day, a Saturday, when she went to court with her husband and finished reviewing file jackets," Wing told the jury, adding, "She did not feel she was being asked about whether at any time she wrote on file jackets" as part of her normal judicial functions.

Wheel then took the witness stand to testify in her own defense. The courtroom had slowly filled in anticipation of hearing her testify, and even the weary jury perked up to listen. Sitting forward, with her hands folded, Wheel described her life as an assistant judge before what she termed "adverse publicity" caused her to lose her position. She recounted in detail how she had fought to defend the position of assistant judge from the "professionals" who wanted to eliminate the position. "The assistant judge's institution has always been under attack. You'd finish one battle and you'd prepare for the next year and the next," she said, adding, "There is a minority group of lawyers and judges who sit in our courts who want to strip the authority of the elected judges."

Davis guided Wheel through what was no doubt carefully-scripted testimony. She described being shown "very bad photocopies" of files during the inquest and told the jury she never put her signature on any file folder jacket "outside of my normal judicial function." She said, "I was never shown the original file jackets, I was never shown the contents of the files. I was never allowed to look at them." Asked at one point, "Did you put your name on any of those file jackets, or initial them in any way?" Wheel's response was a defiant, "Absolutely did not, did not." Davis asked Wheel if she had any knowledge of the investigation into her pay vouchers before the investigation became public in late December, 1985. Wheel's answer, "As God is my judge, I had none," which put her testimony in direct contradiction to that of Chief Justice Allen. Davis suggested through questioning that Allen had actually called to tell Wheel that a television station, not the attorney general's office, had requested to see her pay vouchers and that there had been no mention of an investigation by the attorney general.

Wheel looked straight at the jury as she portrayed herself as a meticulous official who reviewed every case and every order carefully, who would often spend long hours in her chambers signing legal papers, and who deserved to be paid for those activities. She read a portion of the letter she had sent to the Supreme Court a few days after the pay voucher investigation had become public, in which she suggested that Fee was at the heart of the accusations against her. "I would hate to think that Mr. Fee has tampered with the computer or the records," Wheel had written to the justices, "although that possibility cannot be ignored." Wheel also blasted the press coverage of her case, telling the jury the press hounded her day and night and even had laid in wait outside her house for her. "I lost all freedom of movement. I was subjected to humiliation beyond description. I could not go anywhere in my community without people poking each other and saying, 'There she is.'" She had become a pariah in her own town.

Davis concluded his questioning by early afternoon Wednesday, and Suntag, who had been waiting a long time for this moment, immediately zeroed in on the first count of the charge. Wheel had been asked at the inquest if "there was ever a day or a weekend in 1985 or 1986 when you went to the Chittenden Superior Court to correct some entries on jacket files?" Wheel had testified how she had understood that question to refer only to that one Saturday when she went to the court to review files, and that her answer, "never, never wrote on a jacket," was true because she never wrote on a file that Saturday. That prompted the following exchange, illustrating the tension between these two combatants:

Suntag:   What does the word "never" mean to you.

Wheel:    To answer that would insult the intelligence of the jury.

Suntag:   I'll take that risk, Mrs. Wheel.

Wheel:    I think, simply put, not.

Suntag:   How about "not once"?

Wheel:    Never does not mean not once, not in my opinion.

Suntag responded with more than a degree of ridicule, "Sounds like here 'any time' meant one time, and 'never' meant sometime." Wheel reacted defiantly to Suntag: "No one on this earth, not even you, Mr. Suntag, knows what was in my mind when you asked me that question at the inquest. I testified to the truth as I understood the question, Mr. Suntag."

Wheel told the jury she went to the inquest expecting to be asked about her pay vouchers and was so "shocked" and surprised at seeing the signatures on the file folder that "her mind jumped to that Saturday when she had gone to the court to review files on the advice of her attorney. She testified that she did not write on any file jackets that Saturday and had answered truthfully as she understood the question. However, Suntag was prepared for this explanation. He pointed out to her and the jury that her statement that she "never" signed a file jacket appeared on page 209 of the inquest transcript. The first time she was shown her signature on a file jacket was two pages later, on page 211. In other words, he argued, when she answered "never," she could not have been "shocked" at seeing her signature because she hadn't been shown it yet.

Wheel insisted over and over again that she was shocked from seeing her signature on the file jacket, and hence responded to the inquest question by saying "never, never wrote on a jacket." He and Wheel sparred through the following exchange:

Suntag:   You had not been shown copies of file folders (when you answered "never").

Wheel:    I don't know what you expect me to say.

Suntag:   Mrs. Wheel, we expect the truth.

Wheel:    I am giving you the truth. I am a truthful woman.

Leaning over Wheel, and in a softer voice, Suntag reminded Wheel that a U.S. Postal inspector had testified that the signatures were hers "to the exclusion of anyone else in the world." She repeated her explanation that the only time she ever signed her name to a folder was "in the course of my judicial duties."

As Suntag continued his cross-examination, Wheel's demeanor gradually shifted as she leaned back in her chair, her face pale and tense, her glance now more down than at the jury. She maintained that the chief justice was wrong when he told the jury he had told her about the pay voucher investigation in November 1985. She said that Suskin was wrong when he testified that she told him she and her husband went into the courthouse on Saturdays to correct the files. "Are you telling us, Mrs. Wheel, that Lee Suskin was lying?" Suntag asked. "I'm not suggesting he was lying," Wheel responded, "I'm suggesting that he did not understand what was being said that day."

Wheel also insisted that Victor Fremeau, the custodian at the court house, was mistaken when he had testified that he brought Wheel some files to review in February. She told the jury that Fremeau brought her files to examine in January, not February, and that he was present when she reviewed them. By the end of the day, almost four weeks from when the trial had begun, Suntag ended his cross-examination, and the defense rested its case. McCaffrey ordered the lawyers to be prepared for final arguments on Monday morning, after which he would give the case to the jury to decide.

Monday, February 22, 1988 dawned overcast and bitterly cold as the tired jury filed into the Rutland courthouse to hear closing arguments and finally to decide Wheel's fate. Wheel stared downward as Suntag described how Wheel found herself getting caught up in a web of lies and deceit as she signed her name to the file folders to cover up the fact that she didn't sit on court cases for about a year and then lied about it. "Ladies and gentlemen, the evidence shows she is a liar. But we have never claimed she is a good liar." He accused Wheel of an "Alice in Wonderland view of the world, where words begin to mean only what the person wants them to mean, a world where words like "never" mean "sometimes" and "anytime" means "whatever she wants it to mean."

As Davis approached the jury to give his closing argument, Wheel looked up and put on her glasses, following Davis closely as he portrayed her as an innocent victim, the target of people with vendettas out to destroy the institution of assistant judges, and finally as a victim of the justice system itself. He told the jury that prosecutors used 'suspicion, conjecture and statements taken out of context," declaring that "Jane Wheel did not lie." After urging the jury to "pay attention to the human element," Davis concluded his closing argument with a final plea to the jury, "Remember, Jane Wheel did not lie. She deserves your verdict, which hopefully will return to her some semblance of a normal life, some part of her reputation, her respect and honor, restored."

McCaffrey read the jury his instructions in the case, telling them they should acquit Wheel if they found that she had testified incorrectly at the inquest due to "surprise, haste, confusion, inadvertence or honest mistake of the facts," and he then sent them off to begin deliberations. It would take the jury more than nine hours to announce it had reached a verdict. As they marched in and were seated in the packed courtroom, the jury forewoman, Tina Plucin, stood and announced they had found Jane Wheel guilty on all three counts of perjury. "Is that the verdict reached by each of you?" McCaffrey inquired. "It is," Plucin replied. McCaffrey thanked the jury for its extraordinary duty during the long trial, and as soon as he dismissed them, they raced from the courthouse to a waiting bus without comment. Wheel went into a side office and would later slip out of the court house unnoticed.

Davis met briefly with the press, telling them, "She's crushed. I guess it's the best way to describe it." Amestoy, who had arrived earlier in the day to wait for the verdict with his prosecution team, was pleased with the outcome. "It took us a long time to get this case to trial, but when we got it there, we got the right result," he said, adding, "This is exactly the kind of case the attorney general's office ought to be doing. It was a serious crime and it involved the integrity of the judicial system. Otherwise, the message is, if you're a white collar defendant with a deep pocket, you don't get held accountable for your actions."

A few of the jurors were willing to speak later about their experience in the jury room. One described how there had been a gradual progression toward the verdict, with no strong opposition or split among jurors from the beginning, "We had to really work hard at it to come up with a verdict." Another juror described how the jury did not take an initial poll as they began deliberations, saying, "We went over a lot of evidence, then we decided. It was a gradual coming together." While they discussed how hard it was being sequestered for so long, none of the jurors was critical of the time the trial took, and all seemed to agree that "it was necessary to show both sides."

A few days after the trial, Davis filed a motion asking McCaffrey to set aside the jury verdict and enter judgment of acquittal for Wheel. This was standard practice, but what came next was not. In a 53 page, spiral-bound brief, Davis alleged that the jury was biased in the case against Wheel. He wrote that the clerk had reported that a juror had said to her, in the presence of other jurors, "I don't care what happens to that woman." Davis also alleged that during the jury selection process, one juror said he overheard another juror saying to others on the panel that she believed Wheel was guilty. "This juror admitted that she had made up her mind and no evidence could change it," Davis wrote.

These juror issues had been brought to McCaffrey's attention during the trial, and after interviewing the jurors privately, McCaffrey had declined to declare a mistrial. Attacking that decision in his post-trial motion, Davis used strong words, "Rampant prejudice permeated the entire proceeding. Her constitutional rights were blatantly trampled upon. A gross injustice was perpetrated." McCaffrey gave the prosecutors two weeks to file a response to Davis' motion, and eventually denied it.

## B. HILL FACES THE JUDICIAL CONDUCT BOARD

On an unseasonably warm Monday morning, March 7, 1988, just two weeks after the jury's verdict in Wheel's case, now retired Supreme Court Justice William Hill strode into the Barre District Court to finally begin his trial before the Judicial Conduct Board. Dressed in a light coat, with his wife Grace on one arm, and his daughter Elizabeth on the other, Hill stepped forward to face the charges appearing confident and ready to get the matter behind him. The trial was expected to last two weeks.

Conduct Board hearings are held before a three-member Board panel made up of one judge, one lawyer and one lay member. The panel hears evidence, and then reports to the full Board for a vote on whether to recommend to the Supreme Court that discipline be imposed. Harvey Otterman, a well-respected lawyer from Bradford, was serving as chair of the three-member panel. Other panel members were Superior Court Judge Shireen Fisher and Earle Thompson of Rutland. Although there were fourteen individual counts of misconduct against Hill, the state would focus on three critical areas. One was Hill's alleged attempts to intervene in the attorney general's investigation of the pay voucher irregularities. The second was Hill's close relationship with Wheel, which was alleged to have adversely affected his judicial conduct and temperament. And the third was Hill's participation in hearings at the Supreme Court involving the Hunt case.

Before Board prosecutors called their first witness, Wheel's attorney, Carl Lisman, notified the Board he believed Wheel's constitutional rights would be violated if she were made to testify at Hill's trial. The Supreme Court had already ordered Hill's trial delayed so Wheel could complete her criminal case and testify at Hill's trial without jeopardizing her rights. Now, with her criminal case over, her attorneys pointed out that a motion for a new trial in her criminal case had been filed and that a separate Conduct Board hearing was also still pending on multiple ethics charges against her. Otterman gave Wheel's attorneys until the following morning to submit briefs on why Wheel should not be ordered to testify.

David Suntag, the Board prosecutors' first witness, told the Board panel that following news of the investigation in November, 1985, Justice Hill and two other justices had revised the definition of what constituted "official duties" of assistant judges. He told the panel how the new definition had so enlarged the kind of activities viewed as legitimate judicial work that even "planning a party or mowing the courthouse lawn" might be within the scope of work of an assistant judge, "The effect of the definition had a significant impact on our criminal investigation of Judge Wheel," he said. Suntag testified that the new definition of the duties of assistant judges was not lost on Wheel, pointing out that when he asked her at the inquest in May 1986 the activities for which she thought she should receive pay, she read from the "official duties" definition Hill had drafted. Lisa Auer, Hill's secretary at the Supreme Court, was called to testify that Hill asked her to get Wheel's pay vouchers for him to review. Board prosecutors used Suntag's and Auer's testimony to create a picture of Justice Hill's personal concern about the investigation into Wheel's pay vouchers.

Thomas Lehner, who was clerk of the Supreme Court, testified about the chain of events that occurred after news broke that the attorney general was investigating Wheel's pay vouchers. Attorney General Amestoy had sent the chief justice a letter in late November, 1985, notifying him of the investigation.[43] On December 21, the first newspaper article publicly announced the investigation, and a week later, at Hill's urging, Chief Justice Allen had appointed Justices Hill, Hayes and Gibson to write a definition of what constituted "official duties" that would entitle assistant judges to state pay. Hill wrote the definition, circulated it among the justices, and then sent it, bearing his initials, to all the superior courts around the state. Lehner characterized it as "unusual" for the justices to become involved in writing such a definition, noting that it would normally be court administrators, not the justices, working on such policies.

Lehner also described an administrative meeting in February, 1986, when all five justices met to discuss problems at the Chittenden Superior Court. Normally, protocol at such meetings called for the chief justice to introduce a subject, and then for each justice to give his views, starting with the most junior justice and working up to the chief justice. In this case, however, Lehner testified that Hill, who was the most senior

---

43   See Appendix B: Amestoy letter to Allen.

justice, spoke first, and Hayes and Gibson joined him in pressing for an investigation into the work performance of the clerk, Frank Fee. Lehner told the panel that when Justices Peck and Allen said they didn't view the study as a mission to either exonerate Wheel or vilify Fee, Justice Hayes became angry. "Justice Peck spoke up and said he didn't want to be involved in a witch hunt," Lehner said, and went on to testify that the chief justice "did not want to be part of any effort to create a defense for Jane Wheel." Lehner described Hayes' reaction. "When the Chief Justice said that, Justice Hayes backed his chair away from the table and became very agitated, pointing at the Chief Justice and saying, 'You show me one place, one time, where I've indicated I would be part of a whitewash for Jane Wheel.'"

The first day of hearings in Hill's case was a busy one. Seven witnesses took the stand, including former Attorney General John Easton, who described how Wheel had urged him to provide public support for the power of assistant judges during one of the appeals of the Hunt case to the Supreme Court. He testified that Wheel told him that the assistant judges in Vermont were a "powerful force" and could be "helpful" to his "political future." During the opening day of testimony, Board prosecutors called a number of court employees to describe incidents which, at times, seemed better suited for a soap opera than a courthouse. Joan Girard, the court stenographer, testified about what it was like to incur Wheel's wrath. Girard, one of the "Wheelgate Seven," described how she initially was "one of the few court reporters who could get along with Wheel." She had been assigned a second floor office sandwiched between the offices of Wheel and the presiding judge. She described how Wheel had a practice of leaving all the doors between offices open so she could see from her desk what the presiding judge was doing. "Judge Wheel insisted doors be open all the time," Girard told the panel. "If I ever shut the door for any reason, she would open them back up again." Girard said that Wheel would close her door when she had a phone call or if Hill was visiting with her. She described how, after she testified under subpoena at one of the inquest hearings investigating Wheel, she came to work one day to find her entire office had been moved to the third floor.

Girard also testified to an earlier incident in happier times when Wheel invited her to a social gathering at the Holiday Inn in Waterbury. One day in early 1985 Wheel told Girard that Judge Hayes "had been working very hard lately and needed relief," so she was organizing a group get-together. "When Jane Wheel invited you to do something, you did it,"

Girard said, adding that she couldn't think of an excuse fast enough to get out of the invitation. It was a stormy night, and Girard, who was eight months pregnant at the time, described how, when she called Wheel's home after work to try to get out of the trip, Wheel's husband answered the phone and said Wheel was out attending a meeting in Montpelier that evening. Girard went on to describe how she and her husband arrived at the Holiday Inn on time, and finding no one from the Court there, had dinner by themselves. When she came out of the dining room to see if Wheel was there, she observed Wheel, Hill, and Hayes just arriving arm-in-arm. "Justice Hayes had one arm, and Justice Hill had his arm linked through her other arm," Girard said, noting that, "Wheel danced with Justice Hill that evening. I know they were on the dance floor doing a waltz," then they "stayed on for a faster dance." Girard described how later in the evening a good friend of Hill's, David Putter, a Montpelier lawyer, showed up and joined the group. They all sat around drinking and discussing Judge Hayes' recent application to become a justice of the Supreme Court. When she and her husband did finally leave around 11:00, Hill, Hayes, Wheel and Putter remained. On cross-examination Hill's attorneys did get Girard to say that it was wet outside, and probably slippery, presumably to offer a justification for why the justices came into the Holiday Inn arm-in-arm with Wheel.

A common theme running through all the alleged ethical violations was that Hill had allowed his close relationship with Wheel to interfere with his judicial objectivity and temperament. The state continued to offer more glimpses into the "close" relationship between Hill and Wheel. Margaret Maskell had been a deputy clerk at the Chittenden court for many years and had been friendly with Judge Hill before Judge Wheel came to the Court in 1974. Maskell told the panel of Wheel's intense interest in Hill while he was still a Superior Court judge. She described how Wheel continually asked numerous questions "of a personal nature" about Hill, including whether Maskell had "ever met his wife...Were they happy....What kind of wife was she (since) his ties never matched his coat?" She testified that she and other employees became concerned as they watched Wheel and Hill become closer and closer friends. She said Wheel would speak fondly of Hill in front of the court staff and lavish praise on him in awkward, uncomfortable ways. It got to the point that Maskell described calling Hill to let him know Wheel was talking about him all the time "and you know, people in the office were starting to talk." She denied it was a warning, she just wanted him to know.

Maskell's most damaging testimony came as she described knocking on Hill's office door one day and then entering with an urgent message to find him sitting at his desk, with Wheel leaning over him from behind the chair with her arms wrapped around his neck and shoulders. "Her hands were on Judge Hill...around his neck," she told the ethics panel, adding that she saw Wheel leap back from the chair as Judge Hill screamed at her for entering his office. Hill was furious at her for entering his office. "He called me out," she said, adding that he screamed, "How dare you barge into chambers..." She testified that she broke down in tears as she left. She saw Hill later in the day, she said, and he scolded her again for coming into his chambers.

Maskell also told the panel of another incident when she and a friend were stopped at a traffic light on Main Street in Burlington on a Friday evening. Wheel had announced earlier that day that she was going to Boston for the weekend. Maskell described how, as she and her friend sat at a red light, she saw Hill peer through the window of the bus station, and then saw Wheel come out of the station with a suitcase. "We saw Judge Hill walk up Main Street" to the bus station, she said, adding that "Judge Wheel came out...he took her suitcase and they walked down the road" together with "his arm on her back." She testified that she got a clear view of the two of them, and there was no doubt in her mind it was Hill and Wheel. Hill's attorney's objected to the whole line of questioning, saying at one point, "I am just mystified about how this relates to Justice Hill." Otterman allowed the questioning to continue. Marks did everything he could to shake Maskell's testimony on cross-examination. Maskell could not remember when the event at the bus station occurred, except to say it had been several years earlier, and she admitted she and her friend had been to a bar for a drink earlier. However, she knew what she saw, and she remained strong and confident in her testimony.

The state's claim that Hill and Wheel had an intimate relationship, one that went well beyond collegiality, was a key element in all of the charges against Hill. It was this alleged relationship that the state continued to bolster when Board prosecutors called retired Superior Court Judge John Morrissey as a witness. Morrissey and Hill were friends, and Hill would occasionally stay at Morrissey's house when Hill was in the Bennington area. Morrissey testified that in the early 1980s, he was invited on a ferry ride across Lake Champlain from Charlotte to Essex, New York, for dinner with Hill and Wheel. Morrissey said that Wheel wanted them to meet her son, who was a captain on the ferry boat. The three of them got over to Essex around 4:30 only to find out the restaurant didn't open until 6:00. Morrissey told the Board panel that he decided not to wait and took the next ferry back to Vermont, but that Hill and Wheel stayed to have dinner together. He said he did not know how or when they returned to Vermont.

Morrissey also told the panel that on two occasions Wheel telephoned him at his Bennington home and asked him to call Hill at his home. On one occasion, Morrissey said, Wheel wanted Hill to call her back, and on the other occasion, she asked Morrissey to tell Hill to meet her the next day at "the place." Morrissey also told the ethics panel that, in addition to those two telephone calls, Hill also asked him once to telephone Wheel for him. Morrissey was vague as to when these events happened, but he said had a clear recollection of them. Marks attempted to chip away at the edges of all these witnesses, but their testimony went pretty much unchallenged on cross-examination. Marks did ask Morrissey if he felt Hill and Wheel had an intimate relationship. "None that I recall," Morrissey responded.

John Morrissey has his own sad place in Vermont's judicial history. He was appointed to the superior court bench in 1974 by Governor Salmon, and while he was generally considered an excellent judge, he had his own demons. He pleaded no contest in 1976 to a charge of drunk driving, and in 1979 his driver's license was suspended after a second such plea. In 1983, he was driving the wrong way on Interstate 89 and his automobile collided head on with another vehicle. Donald H. Hackel, president of the Vermont Bar Association and a friend of Morrissey's, emphasizing that he was speaking personally and not as a bar official, said of Judge Morrissey: "He has a deep sense of responsibility. He might well feel obliged to step down." Morrissey resigned from the bench in 1983 shortly after the accident. He died in June 2008 at the age of 78.

The second day of Hill's trial opened with some dramatic testimony by Superior Court Judge James Morse, who described how "low" morale had become at the Chittenden courthouse in 1984 and 1985. Morse described the Burlington courthouse as "the most unhappy place I ever worked. People had very, very low morale. There was a lot of fear being exhibited by just about everybody I talked to." When asked by Board prosecutors why that was the case, Morse's terse response was, that "[t]he personnel there feared Jane Wheel." Hunt's attorney at his murder trial, Robert Gaston, described the complicated history of the Hunt case. He told the panel how Wheel had gone directly to Hill for help after Morse had disqualified her from the case. He described how Hill, acting on his own and contrary to the Court's own procedures, overruled Morse's disqualification of Wheel, and then took the case away from Morse and had it transferred to another county to save Wheel from embarrassment.

Another important ethics charge against Hill alleged he had inappropriately interfered with the Wheel investigation when he personally delivered the letter to Attorney General Amestoy expressing the Supreme Court's "deep" concern over how long the Wheel investigation was taking and about the leaks of information. Amestoy would later describe how his secretary came into his office to tell him that Supreme Court Justice Hill was on his way to personally deliver something. He was stunned. He didn't know what it was about, but "he knew it was not to congratulate him." Amestoy had only been attorney general a short time at that point, and later admitted to being a bit unnerved as he sat waiting for Hill to arrive. His instincts were to ask his deputy, Brian Burgess, to sit in on the meeting, but then again, this was a justice of the Supreme Court who wanted to meet with him. Burgess told Amestoy that the walls were paper thin and that he could often hear conversations from his office next door. Burgess found a screw driver and hammer and punched a small hole in the wall between their offices. As Hill delivered the letter to Amestoy and sat staring at him while he read it, Burgess had his ear pressed to the hole in the wall.

Amestoy testified that after reading the letter, he told Hill he would reply in writing. As Hill left the office, he turned to look back at Amestoy and told him "that it would not be advisable to release this letter publicly." Hill apparently enjoyed his moment of confronting the attorney general. As Hill left the office, Assistant Attorney General Marilyn Skoglund came into Amestoy's office and asked, "What have you done to make Justice Hill so happy?" Amestoy said, "I didn't think I had done anything to make him happy." Skoglund, who herself would later become a Supreme Court justice, said, "He just went by me, threw his arms open and said, 'It is a beautiful day,' or words to that effect."

Amestoy told the panel he was concerned about the letter being delivered so soon after the Court had taken action adopting the new definition of official duties of assistant judges. "So when I received the letter, I was concerned it was a less than an objective expression of concern," Amestoy said, adding that the letter cast a "cloud" over the Supreme Court. "I was aware of Justices Hill, Hayes and, to a lesser extent, Gibson's relationship to the defendant," Amestoy said, adding, "I read the letter as a not-so-subtle message to me that this investigation would be better completed and completed quickly."

The big news of the day on Tuesday, March 9, however, came from testimony that didn't happen. Board prosecutors called Wheel to the witness stand, and her attorneys announced that she would refuse to testify. They continued to argue that she had to assert her Fifth Amendment rights to protect the appeal of her criminal conviction and not to jeopardize her own Conduct Board hearing. The Board advised Wheel that she must testify about the conduct board matters, even if they "might embarrass her or prejudice" her in her own conduct board hearing.

Wheel took the stand and answered some preliminary questions, but when asked by Board prosecutors about her relationship with Hill, Wheel said, "Upon advice of counsel, I respectfully decline to answer this question on the grounds that such answer might incriminate me." Otterman responded by telling Wheel, "Our determination would be that the question is indeed relevant and proper, that the Fifth Amendment privilege does not entitle Judge Wheel to decline to answer and that we view her refusal to answer as a violation of our specific direction to do so." She was asked another question: "During 1984 and 1985, were you in the habit of going to the Holiday Inn lounge on Friday afternoons with Justice Hill, Judge Hayes, and Francis Fee and talking about court business?" Wheel repeated her Fifth Amendment claim, and Otterman repeated his directive that she must answer. She again refused.

Board prosecutors then outlined more than forty areas about which they wanted to ask Wheel, including "all aspects of her relationship with Hill," bickering between Wheel and various court employees, and a number of actions, some allegedly undertaken with Hill's assistance, done to bolster her position in the courthouse. Wheel announced that she would assert her Fifth Amendment right with respect to all the questions. Otterman told Wheel the Board would ask the Supreme Court to find her in contempt for refusing to answer questions. Davis responded by advising Otterman and the other panel members, "I don't think we're risking contempt. If asserting one's right not to testify under the Fifth Amendment presents a risk in this country, then we better start with a new system."

Hill's trial continued Thursday with a list of witnesses describing tales of intrigue, obsession, and intimidation at the Chittenden courthouse. In three hours of sometimes emotional testimony, Frank Fee painted a picture of a courthouse filled with turmoil and of an assistant judge who had "always gotten her way." He described how Wheel forbade him from going to lunch with retiring Justice Wynn Underwood. "I do not want you to go out to lunch with this man. He is an enemy of mine and of assistant judges," he said Wheel told him. When he told her he had no choice, Wheel said, "As my clerk, I forbid you to go to lunch with that man." Fee testified that after he went to lunch with Underwood, Wheel stopped talking to him.

Fee described a meeting in October 1985 in which Justice Hill had summoned him to the Supreme Court. He described the meeting as lasting almost two hours, and while Justice Hayes looked on, Hill berated Fee for the problems at the Chittenden courthouse. Fee told the panel how Wheel had wanted one of the scheduling clerks at the court fired, although attorneys and other judges said she was doing an outstanding job, and at the meeting, Hill pushed Fee to fire the clerk. Fee described the social atmosphere that existed in the courthouse despite the tensions in the day-to-day operations there. He said that he often went with Hill, Wheel, and Hayes to the Holiday Inn in Burlington for drinks two or three Friday nights a month. He told the ethics panel that they discussed a variety of subjects, including matters pending before the court. Fee said that he could recall one or two occasions where they discussed Judge Morse's disqualification of Wheel from sitting on the Hunt case. He also said there were discussions about changing the venue of the Hunt case to another county.

Supreme Court Justice Wynn Underwood had spent several years as a superior court judge in the Chittenden courthouse before his appointment to the Supreme Court. He described how, before Fee took the Clerk's position, he had tried to warn him just what he was getting into. Underwood, who was a soft-spoken, highly regarded jurist, testified that he told Fee "how much interference he might have from the assistant judges in carrying out his duties." Underwood said he warned Fee, "With Judge Wheel, you had to very careful. She was oversensitive about certain matters...I had to handle her with kid gloves."

Board prosecutors called William Nelson, the appellate attorney who had represented Gordon Hunt in his appeals to the Supreme Court, to testify about his experience appearing before Justice Hill in the Hunt case. The three-member Board panel heard a 25-minute tape of the hearing before the Supreme Court in which an extremely emotional Justice Hill had interrogated Nelson and Assistant Attorney General Susan Harritt. Nelson told the Board that Hill's "apparent anger" at the hearing "made me very suspicious. It made me wonder where Justice Hill was coming from. I more or less decided I would have to make a motion to have Justice Hill disqualified."

Board prosecutors used a break over the weekend to file a motion asking the Supreme Court to hold Wheel in contempt for refusing to answer questions before the Conduct Board. "Judge Wheel made a binding pledge before trial that she would testify voluntarily at the Hill hearing if only those hearings were postponed until after her own trial," Board prosecutors wrote in their motion to the Court. "Here it would be unconscionable to permit Judge Wheel to continue to manipulate our judicial system for her own devices." The Court was asked to send Wheel to jail for 90 days. The Conduct Board's own attorney, Alan George, offered a possible compromise to resolve the stalemate over whether Wheel should testify. He asked the Supreme Court to consider granting Wheel immunity from prosecution for any testimony she might give before the Board. "What that would do for us is to make it possible for Judge Wheel to testify without fear that she would incriminate herself," George wrote in a motion, adding, "It's a practical solution to the problem." The Supreme Court took the matter under advisement and ordered oral arguments on the issue for the following morning.

Hill's trial continued in the Barre courthouse, with a parade of witnesses that included some of the state's top judicial officers, including Superior Court Judge Stephen Martin, Chief Justice Frederic Allen, and Supreme Court Justice Louis Peck. Peck was a reluctant witness, volunteering little about Hill and the inner workings of the Supreme Court. Some of Peck's testimony, however, contradicted earlier statements by Hill. For example, Hill had maintained that he, Hayes and Gibson had wanted to "invite" Attorney General Amestoy to the Supreme Court to have him explain why his investigation was taking so long. Justice Peck testified that was not accurate and explained that the idea of having Amestoy come to a meeting was rejected on a vote of 3 to 2, with Gibson siding with Allen and Peck. Peck testified that a compromise was then reached in which the justices agreed a letter would be sent to Amestoy. The fact that Justice Gibson refused to go along with Hill and Hayes in their desire to summon the attorney general to appear before the Supreme Court was significant, and may have contributed to the prosecutor's decision ultimately to let Gibson settle the claims against him and avoid trial on the charges.

When asked on direct examination whether the letter to the attorney general was from the full court, Peck initially said yes, but then added this: "I have to say that I think both the chief justice and I didn't think very much of the thing in general, but that's not to say we didn't go along with it. It was sort of a, as I understood it, it was sort of a compromise between what Justice Hill and Justice Hayes suggested and the balance of the court." Peck also characterized Hill's questioning of Harritt and Nelson as unusually harsh. "I think it was perhaps the strongest questioning or comment I've ever heard since I've been on the bench and possibly since I've been in the bar," Peck noted.

Peck's testimony was followed by that of Chief Justice Allen, who also contradicted some of Hill's testimony. Hill had testified that he was authorized to sign the letter to Amestoy on behalf of the entire Court, as Allen was on vacation. Allen agreed that Hill was authorized to sign the letter, but he also testified that he hadn't seen the final draft and didn't like it because it appeared to attribute the leaks from the inquest to the attorney general's office and to put pressure on the attorney general. Allen said he would have written it differently, and when asked by Marks on cross-examination if it was fair to say the letter was from the entire court, Allen responded, "No, I don't think so."

The chief justice also contradicted some of Hill's statements surrounding the drafting of the definition of "official duties" of assistant judges. Allen did say that he had appointed Hill, Hayes, and Gibson to draft the definition because they, unlike Justice Peck and himself, had all sat as judges on the trial courts, and they were most familiar with the role of assistant judges. However, Hill had stated that the definition of "official duties" was promulgated in a meeting of the entire Supreme Court, and that he was authorized to send it to superior court judges. Allen testified that there was never a formal meeting promulgating the definition and that Hill sent it out after he had apparently determined that some general consensus had been reached. Allen also echoed Justice Peck's feelings about the abusive nature of Hill's questioning of the attorney's in the Hunt case.

Finally, Chief Justice Allen testified that "on at least two occasions," Hill told him that he was opposed to the Court's sending a letter to the Judicial Conduct Board asking the Board to investigate possible misconduct by Wheel. The chief justice had drafted a letter to the Judicial Conduct Board on behalf of the Supreme Court's asking for an investigation and had circulated it to the other justices for their signatures. That letter had somehow mysteriously become "lost," forcing the chief justice to announce to the other justices that he was sending a new letter to the Conduct Board under his own signature.

On Wednesday, March 16, 1988, a day after oral arguments on the issue, the Supreme Court affirmed the Conduct Board's decision ordering Wheel to testify at the Board hearing. In doing so, the Court granted Wheel limited immunity, meaning that the state could not use any of her testimony against her in any later criminal proceeding.[44] George, the Board's attorney, was pleased with the Court's decision. "This is exactly what the panel wanted," he said, "Hill will now have his hearing run its course in a deliberative way without interruption." With that hurdle finally cleared, Board prosecutors announced that Jane Wheel would be called to the witness stand the next morning.

It had been a long time coming. Seated at the defendant's table, retired Justice William Hill sat back in his chair as he prepared to hear Wheel describe their relationship. Board prosecutor William Donahue wasted little time getting right to the point.

Donahue: Describe your relationship with Hill?

Wheel:     One of collegiality, one of mutual respect.

Donahue: Was it a close relationship?

Wheel:     It was a working relationship.

Donahue: Was it a closer relationship? Did you have a relationship as close as a man and woman can have?

Wheel:     I don't understand that.

At this point Wheel's attorney, Carl Lisman, jumped up, saying, "Let's lay the cards on the table. That's what this case had been about since the very beginning. I think you should ask her."

Chairman: I think you should ask her.

Donahue: Did you have an affair with Justice Hill when he was on the Supreme Court bench?

Wheel:     No.

Donahue: Did you have an affair with Justice Hill when he was on the Superior Court bench?

Wheel:     No.

Donahue: Did you have a secret trysting place when he was on the Superior Court?

Wheel:     No.

Donahue reviewed with Wheel the testimony of the previous witnesses, all of whom had spoken about the close social and personal relationship

---

44  *Hill v. State of Vermont*, 149 Vt. 431

Wheel had with Hill. Wheel leaned forward in her seat, clasped her hands in front of her, and denied it all.

Wheel testified that Hill was "short" and "caustic" with her when she was first elected, and, while they eventually became collegial, she said she took pains to distance herself from Hill and dealt with him mostly in his capacity as an assigned "liaison" with the Chittenden court. Wheel denied that Maskell ever walked into Hill's chambers and saw her with her arms around Hill. She denied ever meeting Hill at the bus station with a suitcase. She denied that she ever discussed the Hunt case with Hill, and claimed she only made "sporadic" visits to the Holiday Inn for drinks with Hill, Hayes and Fee. She denied that she ever called former Judge Morrissey looking for Hill. She denied that she had become angry at Lee Suskin at a meeting at which he failed to criticize Frank Fee. The *Rutland Herald* noted earlier in an editorial that:

> Someone is lying, simply lying. And all the Board's dozen witnesses were officials in the judicial system. Choosing a liar among them will be the Board's sorry task. "Justice," in the dictionary, draws on such words as "fairness," "validity," and "rightfulness" for its definition. But now black-and-white testimony reveals that those qualities stopped at the courtroom door, and worse, that they may have been missing in the courtroom itself. [45]

In the end, Wheel's testimony contradicted the testimony from Morrissey, Suskin, Martin, Fee, Maskell, Girard, Lavallee, Allen and Morse. During cross-examination, Wheel had difficulty remembering much of anything, answering "I can't recall" to dozens of questions, particularly about conversations and interactions with court employees. She did acknowledge that at various times she had no communication with Fee, or with Delaney, or with Girard, or with Suskin, or with Morse, but she testified in every instance it was those individuals' refusal to speak with her, not her refusal to speak to them. And with that, Wheel was excused as a witness.

The courtroom in Barre was tense on Friday morning, March 18, 1988, as Justice Hill, with his wife and daughters looking on, took the witness stand to answer to the misconduct charges against him. Wheel's dramatic testimony the day before had taken some of the anticipation out of Hill's testimony. Indeed, Hill began his testimony by reiterating Wheel's

---

45   Editorial, *Rutland Herald*, March 8, 1988

testimony that initially he and Wheel were not even friends. The assistant judges elected before 1975 were largely a passive group, Hill said, but those elected after 1975 had "a new approach to the office." Wheel was one of a new, younger group of assistant judges who were "aggressive about their relationship with the judiciary," Hill said, adding that, after a year or so, "We had a truce. We had to try to get working together without animosity."

Hill was to spend almost six hours on the witness stand that Friday as his attorney led him through questions regarding each of the misconduct counts. Seizing the moment from Wheel's earlier testimony, Hill's attorneys chose to ask him directly.

> Lisman:   Did you ever have an affair with Judge Wheel?
>
> Hill:     No.
>
> Lisman:   Were you ever sexually intimate with Judge Wheel?
>
> Hill:     No.
>
> Lisman:   Did you ever go away with Judge Wheel overnight or for a weekend?
>
> Hill:     No.

Echoing much of Wheel's testimony, Hill denied Peggy Maskell ever came into his chambers to find him with Wheel's arms around him, and he denied that he ever berated Maskell. He also denied ever meeting Wheel at the bus station and offered as a possible explanation that he had two daughters living in Boston at the time and would occasionally pick them up at the bus station. "If I was with anyone at the bus station at that period, I was with one of my daughters," he said. Hill testified that the relationship with Wheel did not involve calling her at home or visiting her house, and he denied that Morrissey ever called him with a message from Wheel to call or meet her. When asked how he would account for Morrissey's testimony that he had placed calls to him on behalf of Wheel, Hill responded, "I can't."

Hill also denied that he ever discussed the Hunt case with Wheel or talked about it in Wheel's presence and that the subject of the Hunt case never came up during the many Friday afternoon gatherings with Wheel and Fee at the Holiday Inn. Hill also testified that he never considered recusing himself on matters that came before the Supreme Court involving Wheel, including the Hunt case. "I had no relationship with Wheel that was sufficient for me to recuse myself," Hill told the ethics panel.

Hill described his version of the behind-the-scenes drama that played itself out among the five justices as the Wheel investigation dragged on and drew more and more public attention. He denied that his intent was to affect the attorney general's investigation negatively by urging the Court to request that Amestoy explain why the investigation was taking so long. Instead, he said he was concerned about the impact the investigation was having on his colleague and friend, the now deceased Justice Hayes. "The morale of the judges was slipping badly and, more particularly, I had a personal concern in that I was watching one of my best friends become deeply affected by the newspaper publicity, and I'm talking about Justice Hayes," Hill told the panel. He described how Justice Hayes had been "getting paranoid about the fact that every day, almost, there would be articles in the *Rutland Herald* and *Burlington Free Press*" about the investigation, including allegations Wheel had used county funds to throw a farewell party for Hayes when he was elevated to the high court. Hill said Hayes became convinced people were "out to get not only Judge Wheel, but out to get him. It was like Chinese water torture—every day, every day, every day."

Hill described the meeting of the five justices at which Hayes made the motion that the Court ask Amestoy to appear before the Court to explain the delay and leaks in the investigation. The motion was defeated when three of the justices—Allen, Peck and Gibson —voted no. Hill testified that the negative vote provoked an angry response from Hayes. "He said some very unkind things about the rest of us and stalked out of the room," Hill said, adding that "[t]he kindest word was 'gutless'...We stayed in a state of shock." Hill testified that it was after Hayes "blew up" at the meeting that Allen suggested a letter be sent to Amestoy.

Justice Gibson was later called as a witness, and testified that, as former trial judges, it was entirely proper for Hayes, Hill, and himself to draft a definition of official duties for assistant judges, noting that it was an effort supported by the chief justice. Gibson said he also felt the Wheel investigation had taken too long and that he had supported contacting the attorney general about it. "It was something being reported, almost daily, it was casting a cloud over the judiciary," Gibson, said, adding that he had opposed having Amestoy appear before them. "I think it could have been appropriate, but I was concerned that such an invitation may have been misconstrued," he said. Gibson also supported Hill when asked about Hill's questioning of the attorneys in the Hunt murder case, testifying that the questions from Hill "were proper to be asked."

The final day of hearing would not produce any new or dramatic testimony. Hill's lawyers were largely done presenting their defense to the charges, although they spent an hour Monday morning reading from a deposition Hayes had given earlier in the investigation, in which Hayes had noted serious problems with the clerical systems at the Chittenden court. This supported Hill's claim that he was involved at the Chittenden court to correct problems there, not to bolster Judge Wheel's stature in the courthouse. Board prosecutors countered this argument by calling Diane Lavallee, the Chittenden court deputy clerk, who read from a five page memorandum Judge Hayes had asked her to type. The memorandum recommended improvements in scheduling, telephone logs, and related administrative matters. Lavallee testified that Hayes told her he did not believe the recommendations were necessary, but he was writing the memo solely to please Wheel. "He did not feel this was true, but it was to 'satisfy Judge Wheel,'" Lavallee told the panel, adding, "Those were his exact words. I remember where I was sitting when he told me that. He said "only give a copy of it to Judge Wheel and Frank Fee, no one else."

After almost two weeks of dramatic testimony, the Conduct Board panel gaveled the Hill proceedings closed on March 27, 1988. Lawyers on both sides were given time to submit proposed findings of fact and supporting memoranda. The hearing panel reported its findings to the full Board, which in September 1988 adopted the panel's findings and conclusions that in five of the fourteen counts there was sufficient evidence to prove that discipline was appropriate. The Board reported its findings to the Supreme Court, but declined to make a recommendation on a specific sanction.

It is fair to say that both sides were unhappy with the Board's recommendations. Significantly, the Board had found there was sufficient evidence to conclude Hill had committed five violations of the Judicial Code. If sustained by the Supreme Court, Hill would become the first Vermont Supreme Court justice ever found to have violated his ethical obligations. On the other hand, the Board's prosecutors strongly felt that the evidence they had presented supported a finding of violations of several more misconduct counts, and they were outraged by the Board's recommendation to dismiss many of the alleged violations. Hill elected to appeal the Board's finding and recommendations to the Supreme Court. In an interesting twist, the Court asked Hill's lawyers and the Board's prosecutors to address in their briefs whether the Board's prosecutors had standing to argue that more ethical violations should have been found than had been recommended by the Board.

# PART FOUR

*Crimes and Punishments*

## A. WHEEL'S SENTENCE AND APPEAL

Judge McCaffrey announced that the sentencing of Jane Wheel on her conviction on three counts of perjury would take place on Monday, June 13, 1988, some three years after allegations of improprieties had first surfaced. Wheel's attorneys immediately asked McCaffrey to delay the sentencing. They told the judge they needed more time to investigate a possible link between the charges against Wheel and recent allegations that Frank Fee had misappropriated county funds. "Based on newspaper accounts and counsel's conversations with county treasurer John Fitzpatrick," the lawyers wrote, "we are informed and believe that the alleged misappropriations by Mr. Fee extend back to mid-1985." Wheel's lawyers wrote in their motion to McCaffrey that:

> "Frank Fee accused Judge Wheel of misapplication of passport funds and of filing false pay vouchers. We believe it is important that the defense be allowed a reasonable period of time prior to sentencing in which to attempt to uncover facts that may be relevant to both the credibility of the defendant's accusers and which may shed new light on the time frame in which the subject file jacket entries (seeking pay) were signed and who signed them."

As this latest development was playing out in court, Fee announced he was resigning as clerk of the Chittenden Superior Court. He was adamant that his resignation was not connected to his relationship with Wheel or other court problems. He had served as clerk for seven years and said he had made the decision to resign after suffering a heart attack a month earlier and spending ten days in the hospital. "Personally, it's been a rough six years for me," Fee said, noting that his wife had died of leukemia in 1982, leaving him to care for their two teenage children. "It was no secret there was a year or two of difficulty at the court concerning Assistant Judge Wheel," Fee said, but added that "I have no bitter feelings at all. I had never intended to be county clerk forever."

The state opposed any delay in sentencing, arguing that Fee had not testified at Wheel's trial, and that the use of passport funds to fund the party for Judge Hayes had not been an issue at Wheel's trial. Suntag said that even if all the allegations against Fee were true, it would not affect the Wheel case. "You need a little more than that to affect the trial," Suntag argued. Ruling from the bench, McCaffrey denied Davis' motion to delay sentencing. While Wheel's attorneys would eventually get her sentencing postponed two weeks after telling McCaffrey she had a continuing medical problem, on Monday morning, June 27, 1988, Jane Wheel walked into the Rutland District Court surrounded by her attorneys, friends and supporters, to learn her fate. She faced a maximum sentence of 45 years in jail.

The sentencing hearing lasted six hours, and like most other aspects of this case, it was anything but ordinary. A sentencing hearing is an opportunity for a defendant to have family and friends testify on their behalf in support of a lenient sentence. Several prominent elected officials testified on Wheel's behalf, including State Senator Esther Sorrell, who testified that none of the women in their circle could believe the charges. Mary Hartigan, a former Vermont Democratic Party national committeewoman, and Leonard Wing, her previous attorney and former president of the Vermont Bar Association, also expressed disbelief that Wheel could have lied under oath. Vermont's Treasurer Emory Hebard told the judge, "Course I don't believe she lied under oath." None of these individuals had attended the trial, but all described how they believed Wheel was the victim of a two-part vendetta, a victim of liberal democrats in Burlington, like Phil Hoff, warring against a conservative democrat like Wheel. They also described Wheel as a victim of a fight between supporters of the assistant judge system and those who wanted to do away with it.

Wheel's pre-sentence investigation had been conducted by probation officer Paul Hammond, who described speaking with Wheel for several hours on three separate occasions during his investigation. On the other hand, Hammond did not talk at length about the case with either Amestoy or Suntag and had spoken with investigator Randall Moran for only ten minutes. It quickly became clear from Hammond's report and testimony that his sympathies were with Wheel. For one thing, his report and testimony seemed to go well beyond the normal role of a probation officer conducting a pre-sentence investigation. He took particular note of Wheel's "excellent background" and described her as "well thought of in the community," someone who "was never before known to do anything wrong." Hammond testified that he had not read a transcript of the case but had based his testimony on his reading of a synopsis of the case prepared by Wheel's attorneys and from his interviews with Wheel. Hammond appeared to ignore the fact that a jury had convicted Wheel. "I have problems myself...about this conviction. I would certainly have had a difficult time convicting her," he told McCaffrey, adding, "Only God is to be the judge on whether she is guilty or not. She was very convincing to me." Recommending against any jail time, Hammond told McCaffrey he concluded that "this woman had suffered enough," and, calling for leniency, recommended that "a good number of hours of community work would satisfy" the interests of justice. It was curious testimony from a probation officer for a defendant convicted by a jury of three serious felonies.

Wheel was the last to speak, and she remained defiant to the end. Standing erect and speaking in a strong, steady voice, she proclaimed her innocence, telling the judge, "I maintain that I am totally innocent of these charges...It was as Senator Hoff admitted...a political vendetta...I was a victim of selective prosecution...Let history record that the political system has been used." Calling her detractors who were quoted anonymously in news stories as "cowardly, nameless, faceless assassins," Wheel told the court that the attorney general's investigation of her case was "a marathon of unethical practices" and compared her ordeal to the Salem witch trials and the McCarthy hearings. "Little did I know how my answers would be misconstrued and distorted," she said, adding that, "the judicial system has been used for a political purpose."

When the state finally had its opportunity, Suntag told the judge that the maximum penalty for a crime was a good indication of its seriousness, and noted that treason was the only non-violent crime with a higher maximum penalty than perjury. He told McCaffrey that Wheel should stop blaming everyone else. "The defendant has had her full day in court and has been convicted," he said, adding, "She held a position of trust. She engaged in a contemptuous violation of that trust." Saying that he believed jail time was warranted, Suntag asked McCaffrey to sentence Wheel to one to three years in prison.

After a brief recess to consider the arguments and testimony, McCaffrey returned to a crowded, quiet courtroom. He began by noting the rarity of one judge passing judgment on another judge and described Wheel's conviction as "an offense which strikes at the heart of our judicial system." Looking directly at Wheel, he said "When the truth is compromised, then the very operation of our government is compromised. This is not a victimless crime. Any breach of trust is serious and affects the very fabric of our society." He also responded directly to Wheel's claim that it was a conspiracy against her. "Too often did we hear terms like vendetta in this hearing, too often did we hear it was someone else's fault," McCaffrey said, telling Wheel that only until a person accepts responsibility for a crime can he or she begin the rehabilitation process.

By this time everyone in the courtroom knew the sentence would be significant. McCaffrey was known to detest abuse of power by public officials, and he told Wheel so. "The thread that seems to run through this case is abuse of power. It is sometimes easy to lose the true perspective of our office." And with that, he ordered Jane Wheel to serve a one- to three-year prison sentence, with forty-five days to be served in jail, and she was to be on probation for the remainder of her sentence. She was also ordered to perform 1500 hours of community service for the elderly, homeless, and female prisoners in Vermont. McCaffrey told her he hoped it would help to restore her standing in the community. Suntag was satisfied with the sentence, noting that "When a judge commits perjury, that's an ultimate violation of that position. That's really what he [McCaffrey] said," adding that he thought the sentence was fair. Even Davis acknowledged, "It could have been a lot worse," he said. Davis filed a notice of appeal with the Vermont Supreme Court, and Judge McCaffrey agreed to let Wheel remain free until the Court ruled on her appeal. Davis expressed confidence in their appeal, but Jane Wheel knew she was headed to the Supreme Court again, this time for the most important matter in her life, and she had no friends left there.

In September 1990, more than two years after a Rutland jury had found Wheel guilty of perjury, the Supreme Court issued its decision in her appeal. The Court was still patching itself together to hear these matters, and for this appeal, Justice John Dooley was again the only regular member of the Court. He was joined by retired Chief Justice Barney, retired Superior Court Judge John Meaker, and two district court judges specially assigned to hear the case, Frank Mahady and Dean Pineles. Justice Dooley wrote the unanimous decision of the Court.[46]

Wheel had argued in her appeal that the new set of "official duties" promulgated by the Supreme Court during the investigation "effectively eviscerated" the investigation and foreclosed any possibility of charging her with misconduct. She claimed that the sole purpose for which the state went forward with the inquest was to entrap her. In rejecting this argument, the Court noted that the state had uncovered evidence indicating that Wheel was involved in a cover-up of her alleged submission of false pay vouchers and that "the scope of the inquest properly included any cover-up activities undertaken by defendant." The Court also rejected the argument that the prosecutor's questions at the inquest were designed to entrap Wheel.

---

46   *State v. Wheel*, 155 Vt. 587 (November 30, 1990)

Wheel also argued that the entire jury panel was "compromised" because they freely discussed their opinions about the case based on what they had read in the newspaper. The Court noted that Judge McCaffrey had interviewed each juror during the trial to determine if the juror could decide the case impartially based on the evidence presented at trial. The Court held that Wheel had failed to demonstrate that the jury panel had a fixed bias against her or harbored preconceived notions concerning the case. "Accordingly," the Court wrote, "we decline to overturn the court's judgment on this point."

Taking another line of attack, Wheel's attorneys argued that the state had conceded she was surprised at the inquest by the questions about her signature on file folders. Surprise can negate the intent to deceive, which is a required element of perjury. Noting that McCaffrey had instructed the jury that it should find Wheel not guilty if it found that she gave incorrect answers to question because of surprise, the Court found there was ample evidence from which the jury could have determined that Wheel was not surprised by the questioning.

The real meat of Wheel's defense was the claim that the evidence at trial simply did not support a guilty verdict. In considering this claim, the Court evaluated the evidence supporting each of the three counts of perjury on which Wheel had been convicted. The first count charged Wheel with falsely swearing that she never added her name on the file jackets to alter the record of her court appearances. The Court reviewed this relevant testimony from the inquest:

Q. Judge Wheel, did there ever come a time when you went through files, a number of files, in Chittenden Superior Court and made some changes on the jacket entries yourself?

A. Never.

Q. Was there ever a day or a weekend in 1985 or 1986 when you went to the Chittenden Superior Court to correct some entries on jacket files?

A. Never. Never wrote on a jacket.

Q. You never wrote on a jacket?

A. Not to correct anything at any time. Reviewed them on the advice of my attorney. I reviewed to get a consensus that I spoke about earlier, but to change, to delete, to add, never.

Q. So any time that you would have written on a jacket entry, it would have been at the time that it was appropriate to put an entry on requested of you by a clerk?

A. It would not have been an entry. It may have just been the judge's initials.

Q. So if your initials are on any jacket files, it's because at the time that the hearing was concluded, for example, or the action was taken...

A. That's very rare; very, very rare.

Q. But the only time you would have done it was at the time it was appropriate to do so?

A. Right there in front of the judge; right there in front of the deputy clerk.

Q. And not some period of time after?

A. Never, never.

Wheel had argued on appeal that the questions were misleading and ambiguous and that, for several reasons, her responses were not false. The Court did not find the questions at all misleading or ambiguous and also pointed out that Wheel's testimony that she had understood the question to refer solely to the Saturday in January when she went to the courthouse to review the files was presented to, and rejected by, the jury.

The second count had charged Wheel with falsely swearing that she did not add her signature to one particular file jacket. The Court reviewed this relevant testimony:

Q. And below that is a –it's hard to see, but it's a signature that says, "Judge Wheel"; does it not?

A. It says that.

Q. Is that your signature?

A. I don't know.

Q. Do you recall ever having written your name on that document?

A. I don't have any recall at all.

Q. The way you explained it before, the only time you would have written on a jacket files, on jacket entries, would have been at the request of the clerk in front of a judge, and you would have put your initials down?

A. It would have been initials.

Q. So not your full name?

A. Never; no.

Q. So, then as we're looking on Page 2, you would not have written your signature in the middle there under the "10/1/85"?

A. Never there; only initials.

Q. So you could not have written your signature here as well?

A. I don't believe I have ever. I have no recall of doing such a thing.

Wheel argued that her conviction on this count should be reversed because she said she was merely stating that she would have written her initials where the signature appeared. The justices had examined the file jacket, leading them to conclude that "the defendant's signature is readily discernible." The Court noted that Wheel had acknowledged the signature said "Judge Wheel," that she could not recall writing the signature, and that she would never write her full signature on a file jacket. The Court held that the jury had sufficient evidence to conclude that Wheel's testimony at the inquest amounted to a false denial that she had signed the file jacket in question.

The third perjury count had charged Wheel with falsely swearing that she did not sign another specific file folder. Again, the Supreme Court reviewed the relevant testimony:

Q. Okay. On Page 3, does this look like –
A. That's a jacket, yes.
Q. And at the bottom there's an entry of "12/20/85," and it had some writing here?
A. Yes.
Q. And then on the bottom left-hand corner, there are two signatures; one says, "Judge O'Day," and one says "Judge Wheel." Is that your signature as Judge Wheel?
A. No, I don't write like that.

Defense counsel argued on this count that there was no evidence that Wheel recognized the signature and thus that the conviction should be reversed. Again, the Supreme Court disagreed, noting that the distinctiveness of Wheel's signature, her awareness of wrongdoing in altering the files, and her motive to cover up the alterations provided more than sufficient evidence for the jury to conclude that she did recognize her signature and then lied it was hers. Finally, the Court considered Wheel's argument that the cumulative effect of all the errors in her case mandated reversal. This was an easy matter for the Court, which declared, "Since we have found no errors, no cumulative effect exists." With that, the Vermont Supreme Court affirmed Judge Jane Wheel's conviction on three counts of perjury.

On Monday, August 19, 1991, more than three and-a-half years after a jury convicted her of lying under oath, Judge Wheel entered the Chittenden Regional Correctional Center to begin serving a forty-five day period of incarceration. The state's archivist, Gregory Sanford, said it was the first jail sentence ever imposed on a Vermont judge. In the end, Jane Wheel would only spend 19 days in the correctional center. The state's jails were overcrowded, and each week prison officials reviewed inmates for possible early release. Wheel had initially been passed over for release because her crime constituted a breach of the public trust. However, Corrections Commissioner Joseph Patrissi said that Wheel also had a medical condition that contributed to the eventual decision to release her early. Patrissi declined to discuss the nature of the medical condition, but he did say that "I certainly didn't want to take responsibility for keeping her inside if she was in a precarious medical state." Wheel was still required to complete 1,500 hours of community service that had been part of her sentence.

Attorney General Amestoy made known his unhappiness with the decision to release Wheel early, arguing that "The message from the corrections commissioner is if you do white collar crime, you won't do the time." Amestoy noted that the jury in Wheel's trial was sequestered for 28 days, during which they were not allowed to go home and were closely supervised by deputy sheriffs, and he added, "It is ironic, to say the least, that the citizens who fulfilled their jury duty in the Wheel case were subjected to a longer period of confinement that the defendant who committed the crime."

Wheel would quietly return to her Burlington home and largely remain out of the public eye. She entered into an agreement with the prosecutors for the Judicial Conduct Board settling her own misconduct case by agreeing not to contest allegations that she violated the ethical Canon providing that a judge "should be patient, dignified and courteous to litigants, jurors, witnesses, lawyers and others with whom (she) deals in her official capacity." The Board said in a statement that Wheel "recognizes that other persons may have perceived her actions as impatient, discourteous or undignified." although her attorney, Leonard Wing, speaking on Wheel's behalf, later commented that "...she doesn't admit anything." In coming to this agreement with Wheel, the Board effectively reduced the multiple ethics charges against her to one, and it explained that the public interest "will be best served if this matter can be concluded without further expense or delay." The Board noted that many of the allegations against Wheel had been fully aired during Hill's trial, and the Board had accomplished its mission to enhance public confidence in the judiciary. The Supreme Court accepted the Board's recommendation and found Wheel guilty of one count of judicial misconduct. It ordered that Wheel be publicly reprimanded, and prohibited from holding judicial office again. It was the harshest penalty that could have been imposed.

Although her ethics case was over, Wheel's criminal attorneys were not yet finished. The day that Wheel entered prison, they brought a *habeas corpus* action in Federal District Court challenging the legality of her imprisonment. They argued to Federal Magistrate Jerome Niedermeier that the state court had erred when it did not make a full inquiry into the conduct of two jurors to determine the fairness and impartiality of the jury. Niedermeier disagreed, finding that the trial court's conclusion that no juror bias existed was sufficiently supported by the record. He also dismissed Wheel's claims that hearsay evidence tainted the jury verdict. Niedermeier recommended to District Court Judge Fred Parker that Wheel's petition for *habeas corpus* be denied. On April 1, 1993, Parker denied the petition.

Wheel was still not done. William Sessions, a prominent Middlebury attorney, filed a notice of appeal of the *habeus corpus* petition to the Second Circuit Court of Appeals. Sessions was a well-known criminal defense attorney who would eventually be appointed a Federal District Judge in Vermont. In her appeal to the Second Circuit, Wheel again argued she was denied a fair trial based on juror bias and prejudice, and that hearsay testimony was improperly admitted that adversely impacted her case. In a decision issued August 25, 1994, the Second Circuit rejected the claims, holding that "the evidence was clearly sufficient to sustain Wheel's conviction for perjury."[47]

One might have thought that the end of the road had been reached. But not so. In a timely fashion, Wheel filed a petition for a *writ of certiorari* asking the United States Supreme Court to take her case. In a one sentence ruling on April 18, 1995, ten years from when the whole sad, sordid story first spilled out into the public, the United States Supreme Court denied Wheel's petition. It was now finally over.

# B. THE SUPREME COURT AND JUSTICE HILL

In September 1989, almost a year following the Judicial Conduct Board's recommendations to the Supreme Court, the Court finally issued its decision in Justice Hill's case.[48] The "special" Supreme Court assigned to hear Hill's appeal of the Conduct Board's findings and recommendations consisted of one sitting Supreme Court justice, John Dooley, one sitting district court judge, George Ellison, and three retired judges—Rey Keyser, Lewis Springer and Albert Barney.

---

47   *Wheel v. Robinson*, 34 F.3d 60 (1994)
48   *In re Justice William C. Hill*, 152 Vt. 549 (1989)

The Court announced that it had used a "clear and convincing" standard in evaluating the evidence, and that it would give great weight to the findings and conclusions of the Board. The Court then addressed the procedural issues Hill had raised, and summarily dismissed claims of political motivations and juror misconduct. Hill was particularly incensed that he had not been given an opportunity to respond to some of the allegations before they were made public, as required by the Board's rules. The Court noted that the Board prosecutors were "in an ambiguous position" because there was no third-party complaint, and they were investigating allegations made mainly in the press. Thus, there were no "specific alleged acts of misconduct before the Board itself filed its complaint." Although the Court found that the rule was not fully complied with, it determined that Hill had received full notice of the charges, had had an opportunity to respond after the complaint was filed against him, and dismissed the claim.

Hill had also argued that because the Board had made egregious procedural errors, the Board's findings and conclusions should be given no weight at all, and the Court should review the facts *de novo*. Since the Court had dismissed all of Hill's procedural claims, it announced that "the findings and recommendations of the Board carry great weight, but they are not binding. The Court is the final arbiter." The Court then turned to review each of the five counts on which the Conduct Board had recommended that Hill be found to have violated the Code. Before doing so, the Court emphasized the high standard of conduct set by the Code of Judicial Conduct. Quoting a Michigan case, the Court stated that "A judge, at any level of the court system, presides at the focal point of the administration of justice. For that reason, a judge must be held to the highest standard of any public official."[49]

# COUNT 19

The Court first turned to review the Conduct Board's findings and conclusion in Count 19, which charged that Hill violated the ethics rules when he signed and personally delivered the letter to Attorney General Amestoy expressing concerns over the length of the Wheel investigation and leaks from an inquest involving the investigation. The Court noted that, for purposes of evaluating this issue, the fact that Hill had personally delivered the letter to the attorney general itself constituted a clear violation of the rules:

---

49   Id, at 373, quoting *In re Callahan*, 355 N.W. 2d 376,386. (1984)

We can think of no purpose to Justice Hill's conduct
except to intimidate the Attorney General. The personal
delivery of the letter, accompanied by Justice Hill remaining while the letter was read, could only convey the
extreme urgency and importance of the matter to Justice
Hill. It was extremely unusual for a justice of the Supreme
Court to initiate a personal contact with an executive
branch prosecutorial officer for purposes of influencing
his actions. It was, beyond argument, an *ex parte* communication concerning an impending proceeding. [50]

Although the Court acknowledged that leaks to the press during
the investigation were affecting public confidence in the judiciary, "the
appearance of Justice Hill's actions went well beyond a good-faith exercise of constitutional responsibilities to protect the judiciary. It necessarily
chilled the Attorney General's action in his responsibility to enforce our
criminal laws." The Court concluded by finding by clear and convincing
evidence that Justice Hill's conduct violated Canon 3A(4) of the Code.[51]

# COUNT 21

This count alleged that Justice Hill violated several provisions in the Code
by participating in appeal proceedings in the Hunt case related to the
disqualification of Wheel from sitting on the case. The Court reviewed
several incidents stemming from Hill's participation in the Hunt case. It
noted that on September 8, 1986 Justice Hill participated in oral argument on the attorney general's motion to withdraw from the Hunt case.
Each member of the Court had listened to the tape of Hill's questioning
of attorneys Harritt and Nelson, and in accepting the Board's recommendation that Hill should have recused himself, the Court wrote that: "It
is apparent to us from Justice Hill's action at that time, particularly the
nature and tone of the questioning and the constant interrupting of counsel, that he was motivated by his anger over the treatment of Judge Wheel
and the hypocrisy he perceived in counsels' actions."[52]

---

50   Id, at 375
51   Canon 3A(4) provides that a judge should accord to every person who is
legally interested in a proceeding, full right to be heard according to law, and,
except as authorized by law, neither initiate nor consider ex parte or other
communications concerning a pending or impending proceeding.
52   *In re Hill*, 152 Vt. at 374

The Conduct Board also had recommended that Justice Hill's harsh questioning of attorneys Nelson and Harriet at the September 8th hearing violated a separate ethics rule requiring a judge to be "patient, dignified and courteous to...lawyers...with whom he deals in his official capacity." In reviewing this finding, the Court noted that "the line between hard and provocative questioning, and impatience and discourtesy, is difficult to draw in an institution built on lively intellectual and adversarial debate" and that "tough questioning does not generally equate to a lack of decorum." The Court held that, although Justice Hill's failure to recuse himself from the hearing violated the Code, it "cannot find by clear and convincing evidence that Justice Hill's conduct during the hearing violated the Code."[53]

A few months later the Hunt case again came before the Supreme Court on a motion that the case be remanded to the lower court for further deliberations. This time Hunt's attorneys had formally moved that Justice Hill recuse himself from hearing the case. He declined to do so, and he had participated in the oral argument. The Court noted that not only could Hill's impartiality "reasonably be questioned," it was being questioned by motions to disqualify him as well as by speculation in the press. "Despite these circumstances, he failed to disqualify himself until faced with a disciplinary investigation," The Court agreed with the Board that "Justice Hill's failure to disqualify himself from all matters involving Judge Wheel by the summer of 1986 and his participation and demeanor during hearings on and after September 8, 1986, constituted a violation of Canons 3C(1) and 3A(4) of the Code of Judicial Conduct."[54]

# COUNT 22

This count alleged that Justice Hill violated several ethics canons by participating in the case to decide whether Wheel should be suspended from acting in a judicial capacity because of criminal charges against her. Despite his lack of objectivity, Justice Hill had participated in the October 6th argument and had forcefully argued that Wheel should continue to

---

53  Id.

54  Canon 3A(4) provided that a judge should be patient, dignified, and courteous to litigants, jurors, witnesses, lawyers and others with whom he deals in his official capacity. Canon 3C(1) required recusal by a judge in a proceeding "in which his impartiality might reasonably be questioned."

be compensated during her suspension. The Court concluded that Hill's participation in the proceeding violated Canons 2A and 3C (1).[55]

# COUNT 23

The Court turned to the Board's recommendation that Hill be disciplined for threatening to retaliate against Nelson, the defense attorney in the Hunt case, if Nelson filed a motion to disqualify Hill from sitting on the case. This count arose out of a conversation that had occurred at a luncheon Hill had with David Curtis, who was serving as the defender general at the time. In that capacity, Curtis supervised Nelson and other criminal defense attorneys doing public defender work. Hill and Curtis were friends, and Curtis had testified at the Board hearing that Hill had asked him whether Nelson was still angry at him following the hearing in the Hunt case. Curtis had responded that although Nelson was not angry, the defender general's office might be filing a motion to disqualify Hill from continuing to sit on matters involving the Hunt case. Curtis testified that Hill's response was that he, too, would then have to file "something." Curtis said he believed at the time that Hill was threatening to file a professional conduct complaint against Nelson if the defense attorneys tried to force him off the Hunt case. Curtis had testified at the Board hearing that the day after the luncheon, he received a telephone call from Justice Hill. Curtis had described his conversation with Justice Hill in questioning from Hill's attorney, Michael Marks:

Curtis: What I remember of the conversation was that Justice Hill indicated he wanted to make sure that I understood that what he had said the day before was basically, his comment was in a facetious manner; he was joking.

Marks: Now, Justice Hill's remark that he would have to file something, do you, on reflection, regard that as a facetious comment?

Curtis: Oh, after having received his telephone call, I believe that it was in fact made in a facetious manner.

Marks: You don't regard it as a serious threat to file an ethical complaint against Mr. Nelson?

Curtis: Not at this point, no. Not after having received that telephone call.

---

55  Canon 2A provided that a judge should avoid impropriety and appearance of impropriety in all his activities.

The Conduct Board had recommended that, even if Hill had made the threat facetiously, it was still a violation of Canon 1 of the Code and had recommended discipline for it.[56] The Supreme Court saw this one differently. Assuming the comments were facetious, the Court declined to conclude it was violation of the Code:

> We do not believe that one isolated incident of facetious conduct between friends violated Canon 1, even in the charged atmosphere that developed during the various investigations being conducted at that time. Realizing the "appearance" of his act, Justice Hill clarified his statement the next day. We do not find the evidence discloses a violation of Canon 1 at the lunch meeting between Justice Hill and the Defender General.[57]

After finding Hill guilty on most of the counts of misconduct on which the Board had recommended action, the Court then turned to the arguments of the Board prosecutors, who were outraged that the Board had not issued findings and conclusions on several more alleged violations. They strongly felt there was more than sufficient evidence to support several additional charges, and that the Board had simply failed to make findings and recommendation on several of the alleged violations. What upset Board prosecutors the most was the Board's recommendation to dismiss Count Twelve, which they argued was "the most serious of all the counts." It alleged that Justice Hill had engineered the change in the definition of "official duties" of assistant judges just a month after the investigation started to protect Wheel. The Board had concluded that Hill was simply discharging his administrative duties responsibly, and had recommended dismissal of the charge. Board prosecutors listed all the evidence that supported a finding that Hill was guilty of violating the Code as alleged. The list of evidence spanned more than six pages in their brief, and told the whole story of how Wheel ran to Hill within a day or two of when questions about her pay vouchers first became public, and how Hill had carefully orchestrated the adoption of the new definition. The Board prosecutors stressed to the Court the impact the new definition had on the attorney general's investigation, pointing out that before the adoption of the new definition of official duties, the attorney general had

---

56 Canon 1 provided that a judge should uphold the integrity and independence of the judiciary.
57 *In re Justice William Hill*, 152 Vt. 548 (1989)

probable cause to believe Wheel had submitted false pay vouchers; after the adoption of the new definition, prosecution on the pay voucher charge was considered no longer viable.

In another instance, Board prosecutors had alleged that Justice Hill had mistreated a court employee, Margaret Maskell, when she had entered his chambers without knocking and found Judge Wheel with her arms around Hill. Board prosecutors quoted the Board's finding that "Hill became angry and admonished her for entering without waiting for a response to her knock, noting that the berating from Justice Hill had made her cry." Although finding these facts to be true, the Conduct Board adopted a very narrow view of the ethics requirement that a judge be "patient, courteous, and dignified to a person with whom he is dealing in his official capacity." In recommending dismissal of this charge, the Board had taken the view that this ethics requirement only applied to the demeanor of a judge when the judge was performing judicial duties in a courtroom setting, and did not reach a judge's behavior with clerical staff. Board prosecutors took strong exception to this narrow ruling, arguing to the Supreme Court that;

> Neither the text of the Canon nor the cases interpreting it confine its directive to the courtroom. The Canon applies explicitly to all persons 'with whom a judge deals in his official capacity.' Unless it can be said that Justice Hill's angry admonishment of Ms. Maskell here was not done in his official capacity, then Ms. Maskell is among those whom Justice Hill was required to treat in a patient, courteous, and dignified manner. The board erred in thinking otherwise.[58]

As it turned out, the Board prosecutors' efforts to get the Supreme Court to look beyond the recommendations of the Board were for naught. The Court explained that the Judicial Conduct Board is an arm of the Supreme Court, and that the Board's role is to evaluate evidence and to make recommendations on charges it believes is supported by the evidence. The Court then had this to say about the role of Judicial Conduct Board prosecutors:

The role of Board prosecutors is to present the Board's

---

58   Board Prosecutor's Brief to Supreme Court in *In re Justice William Hill*, 152 Vt. 548.

position to this Court. Nothing in the Rules allows the Board to contradict its own recommendations when its findings and conclusions are being reviewed by this Court and, in effect, to argue for greater sanctions than it recommended in its final report. It is axiomatic, therefore, that Board prosecutors similarly lack standing to attack the Board's conclusions and to argue that more violations of the Code of Judicial Conduct should be found and that greater sanctions are appropriate than those recommended by the Board.[59]

Because the Court ruled that the Board's prosecutors could not appeal from the Board's recommendations, the Court reviewed only those findings and recommendations of the Board in which they had found violations, and declined to consider any of the ethics charges that the Board had recommended be dismissed. The Court concluded its opinion issuing the following order:

> Justice William C. Hill violated Canons 2A, 3A (4) and 3C (1) of the Code of Judicial Conduct. By Monday, September 25, 1989, at 4:30 p.m., Counsel for Justice Hill and Board prosecutors shall file what information they deem appropriate on the sanction that this Court shall impose. An oral argument on the appropriate sanction is hereby set for Tuesday, September 26, 1989 at 1:00 p.m.

It was the first time in its 209-year history that a justice of the Vermont Supreme Court had been found guilty of violating the Code of Judicial Conduct. The Supreme Court would eventually order that retired Supreme Court Justice William Hill be publicly reprimanded for his misconduct and that he be disqualified from ever sitting as a retired judge. It was the harshest penalty that could have been imposed.

---

59   *In re Justice William C. Hill*, 152 Vt. 548 at 552

# EPILOGUE

How could three, highly-respected Supreme Court justices have allowed this profound breach of ethics to happen? The unusually close relationship Assistant Judge Wheel had with Justice Hill, and his overt actions to protect her, had been going on for several years before the attorney general started his investigation in 1985. As Hill's own attorney told the Conduct Board during the hearing, at the heart of the case was whether Hill and Wheel were or had been in an intimate relationship. The Board's prosecutors felt strongly that the evidence supported a finding that they had a relationship far more intimate than they would admit to, and were livid that the Board failed to sustain that charge.

Hill was a powerful, abrupt, and occasionally gruff justice, probably the least intellectual of the three. It would not be hard to imagine a man with his ego finding solace and strength in Wheel's arms. And Wheel's tight connection to Hill certainly fed her need for status, power, and protection. The fact that both Hill and Wheel denied a sexual intimacy under oath put Board members in a difficult position. If the Board found that Hill and Wheel did have an intimate relationship, it would have meant it thought they had lied under oath when they denied it. If the Board found Hill and Wheel did not have an intimate relationship, the Board would be ignoring an overwhelming amount of circumstantial evidence. In refusing to find an intimate relationship existed, the Board may have elected to take the easy way out because it did not need a conviction on this count in order to take Hill off the bench forever. In one of his many memorable passages, Peter Freyne wrote in his *Inside Track* column about Hill and Wheel after the ethical charges were released:

> Now there are those who would say 'No big deal!" After all, we're still talking about 1974-75, when the spirit of the sixties still lingered and psychologists were telling us over and over it is okay to express your feelings and touch one another. Perhaps Jane and Bill got a little too caught up in the sense of liberation that wafted through society, were working on their hang ups and as a way to release themselves from the bonds of psychosexual blocks decided a little unethical hugging was the way to go.[60]

Justice Hill took several bold steps to protect Wheel without ever appearing to be concerned about any ethical obligations. He rewrote the definition of the official duties of assistant judges so the State couldn't prove Wheel was not "working" when she put in for pay. Even though the Supreme Court refused to uphold the Conduct Board's recommendation finding that those actions violated the ethics code, it was a bold, brazen act in the face of his close relationship with Wheel. He vacated Judge Morse's disqualification of Wheel in the Hunt case on his own without even consulting the other justices or even giving notice to the parties. He personally took the letter from the Supreme Court that he had drafted about his concerns in the Wheel case directly to the attorney general, and then sat there staring while the attorney general read it. He repeatedly participated in hearings in the Hunt case, despite obvious conflicts and specific requests that he recuse himself, and he then abused the lawyers. He even sat in on the hearing to decide whether Wheel would be suspended following the filing of the criminal charges, and insisted she be paid during her suspension. Justice Hill allowed his relationship with Wheel, whatever it may have been, to influence his decisions and judgments in matters involving Wheel, and he paid an enormous price.

Justice Hayes may or may not have had an intimate relationship with Wheel. While there were rumors of such a relationship and plenty of suspicious conduct to suggest one, there was less overall evidence that one existed than as to the Wheel-Hill relationship. Hayes did forcefully deny that he had an intimate relationship with Wheel in the statement he gave to prosecutors before he died (although he admitted to having heard the rumors). I suspect that Hayes' friends got it right. He was a kind and compassionate man. He described himself as having a "listening ear," and he extended it to Wheel when he arrived at the court. Perhaps, like Judge Morse, he had been warned about Wheel—Hoff said at one point that he had warned him. In any event, Hayes allowed himself to be ensnared in Wheel's web, a web that he seemed to almost fear ("When you tell Jane Wheel you are going to do something, you'd better do it"), and certainly regret. Justice Hayes was blinded to his ethical obligations as a jurist. He took certain positions and participated in some hearings and phone calls when he should have known better. It is unfortunate that he died before he could fully answer to the charges against him.

Justice Gibson wasn't a social friend of Wheel's, and it is less clear how he found himself swept up in the controversy. Gibson was generally a soft spoken, very respectful judge. He liked the institution of assistant judges, and was genuinely trying to figure out the substantive issues as the Wheel controversy continued to find its way to the Supreme Court. Gibson also struggled with the relentless newspaper coverage of the investigation, and how it was affecting his colleagues on the Court. His written acknowledgement that some of his actions created an appearance of impropriety was an appropriate outcome for him.

It seems clear from the evidence that Wheel, while a bright, articulate woman, had a seriously flawed personality. She went from gym teacher to becoming an assistant judge sitting in the state's highest trial court, and as Phil Hoff said, she was a person who did not figure out how to use power. She seemed to have little to do with those she perceived below her status and importance, whom she mistreated, abused or ignored. It is telling that there was not one courthouse staff person who spoke well of her when she found herself in trouble. Wheel's large ego came with a paranoia that saw enemies everywhere conspiring against her, even among courthouse employees meeting for coffee. She quickly sorted out among the new judges coming to her court who was going to be her friend. There wasn't much in-between for Wheel, if you didn't warm up to her and become a confidant early on, you were an enemy, and she would often simply stop talking to you.

There is some irony in the fact that it was Wheel's own arrogance and careless comments that triggered the events that led her down this path. She thought Delaney, the other assistant judge, was putting in for pay and not working. She asked the clerk, Frank Fee, to look into it, and she set a trap to try to catch Delaney. Fee didn't find any problems with Delaney's records, but as he looked into it further, he discovered that Wheel herself had been putting in for time on days she did not work. In a scene out of *Law and Order,* in a Burlington parking garage Fee met with Deputy Sheriff McLaughlin with the evidence in the trunk of his car. On yet another occasion, knowing she was under investigation over the pay vouchers, Wheel told Lee Suskin from the Supreme Court that the files in the courthouse were a mess and that she and her husband were going in on Saturdays and "fixing" the files. Suskin went back and told Moran, the attorney general's investigator, who went back to check the same files to see if they had been altered. Sure enough, now Wheel's signature was on several of the files. She had been caught.

Wheel probably was more than a bit surprised at the inquest hearing when she was shown case file jackets that she knew she had altered and was asked if they were her signatures. She had come expecting to be challenged on her pay vouchers, and she must have known almost immediately that she had been caught. At that point, she could have told the truth and admitted the signatures were hers. She might have been caught in a cover-up, but she would probably not have been charged with perjury, and it is unlikely she would have gone to jail. But she denied under oath that they were her signatures, and she was suddenly facing multiple felony charges.

There are some mysteries that remain. What did Justice Barney mean in the earlier *Fienberg* case in which the Court had voted 4-1 to dismiss the ethics charges against Judge Fienberg after he decided to resign from the bench? In his dissent, Barney had accused the majority of being affected by "influences not of record." It was a remarkable comment, which prompted Justice Hill to write a concurring opinion. Why was it "fitting" for Hill to respond to Barney? His doing so suggests a battle had been waging between the justices over the decision, or perhaps over something bigger. One can assume Justice Barney was aware of the relationship Hill had with Wheel, and he may have seen the *Fienberg* decision as one in which Justice Hill was doing Wheel yet another favor by protecting assistant judges who retire from being disciplined. Hill couldn't let Barney's comment go unanswered, lashing back at him:

> The dissent speaks righteously of 'influences not of record' as reason for our decision today. Such vague innuendo does nothing constructive to resolve the problem at hand, especially since Mr. Justice Billings refuses to divulge what strange conspiratorial forces he perceives lurking in the corners of our decision.[61]

We are left to wonder what "vague innuendos" and "strange conspiratorial forces..." were "lurking in the corners...".

Another unanswered question is what happened to the letter Chief Justice Allen had written to the Judicial Conduct Board asking that it investigate Assistant Judge Wheel for possible misconduct. Hill was vocally opposed to the Court sending the letter, and when Allen circulated the letter to all the justices for their review, it got "lost." Allen later announced to the full Court that he was sending a new letter, this time just under his own name. What happened to that first letter? And who paid for all the legal work Wheel received, including a nine month-long investigation, a four week criminal trial, an ethics case at the Judicial Conduct Board, and multiple appeals to the Vermont Supreme Court over a period of almost

---

61    *In re Fienberg*, 139 Vt. 511 (1981)

ten years. Wheel and her husband were of modest, middle-class means. Richard Davis and Leonard Wing were two of the most prestigious and expensive attorneys in Vermont. Wheel's legal fees had to run into the tens of thousands of dollars. It was never clear who paid for her lawyers' services.

It was unfortunate that the Court rejected the Board's recommendation that Justice Hill's aggressive questioning of Hunt's attorney, William Nelson, violated the ethics code. The Court did agree that Hill should have recused himself from that hearing, and that it was a violation of Hill's ethics to have participated in the hearing, but it declined to find that Hill's abusive questioning of the attorneys violated ethical standards. In doing so, the Court set a new low for what constitutes "patient, dignified and courteous" treatment of lawyers in the courtroom.

It is understandable why Attorney General Amestoy and the others who worked so hard to bring Wheel to justice were upset when Wheel was released early from jail. In reality, however, Wheel's life as she knew it was effectively over before then, her proud ego had been effectively crushed. She withdrew from public life, and from all accounts she continued to grocery shop late at night to avoid being seen.

Some would question whether going through all of this had been worthwhile. They would point out that Wheel was never even charged with criminal wrongdoing for the allegations for which she was being investigated. They wondered whether the charges of lying under oath were a "mere technicality," not worth the $100,000 spent to investigate and prosecute a judge who had already lost her election as a result of the charges. Many others would disagree, noting that Wheel's crime was perhaps the most serious for which a judge could be convicted. Commenting on the Wheel case, Ben Aliza, a criminal law professor at Vermont Law School, noted that, "A perjury conviction reflects on the character and honesty of the individual," and he noted that an abuse of the legal system by a judge must be viewed in the context of the high professional standards to which judges swear to uphold.

In the end, the legal community breathed a collective sigh of relief that the long ordeal was over. It took longer than it perhaps should have, but then again, nothing like this had ever happened before in Vermont. Amestoy's decision to pursue the case against Wheel and three sitting justices of the Vermont Supreme Court took courage, placing him in the unenviable position of challenging the integrity of the state's highest court. His willingness to meet with former governor (then state senator) Hoff over the impact the case was having on the judiciary was perfectly proper.

Phil Hoff's approaching Hayes to see whether Wheel would consider not running for re-election was probably ill-advised, but it reflected his deep concern for the impact the evolving scandal was having on the high court and judiciary. Throughout the case, Amestoy was particularly sensitive to charges that he was pursuing the case for political gain, and he was careful to withhold comment on the case.

Amestoy himself would be appointed in 1994 to be chief justice of the Vermont Supreme Court and would serve in that position until 2004. David Suntag would be appointed to the superior court in 1991, and retired in 2015. Justice Gibson remained on the Vermont Supreme Court until he retired in 1997. John Dooley would continue to sit as a Supreme Court justice for 30 years, and retired after a distinguished career in 2017. Leonard Wing continued to vigorously defend clients up until his death in 2005 at the age of 82; a year later, a mediation room at the Rutland court was named in his honor. Richard Davis continued to represent criminal defendants aggressively until his death in 1993.

Both Hill and Wheel were given the maximum punishment permitted by law for their breaches of trust, and both would slip quietly into obscurity. Hill died of lung cancer in May, 1998 at the age 81. Wheel died in March 2017. She was 84 years old. Her obituary never once mentioned her twelve years as an assistant judge.

Time has healed most of the wounds from these sad events, and as memories fade, it cannot be said there has been any lasting damage to the integrity of Vermont's judicial system. Indeed, there is some evidence that going through this experience made the judicial system stronger. Until this point, the Judicial Conduct Board had largely been reactive, responding only when a member of the public filed a complaint about a judge. In this case the Board acted on its own initiative, charging Supreme Court justices with multiple ethics violations, and in doing so, established itself as a pro-active watchdog protecting the integrity of the Vermont judiciary. The Conduct Board's annual report for 2016 noted that the Board had received forty new complaints over the previous twelve months. Most involved citizens unhappy with the results of their case, and were dismissed after an initial inquiry. One judge was issued a private warning, and one case resulted in a contested hearing. In that case, an assistant judge was removed from the bench after being found to have defrauded an elderly woman in his care.[62]

---

62   *In re Assistant Judge Paul Kane*, 2017 Vt. 48

The Supreme Court took the opportunity in the Hill case to remind the judiciary and bar that a judge

> "must conduct himself in such a way that the public can perceive and continue to rely upon the impartiality of those who have been chosen to pass judgment on legal matters involving their lives, liberty and property. For that reason, a judge must be held to the highest standard of any public official."[63]

The Court noted that the reach of the ethics code extends to judges' non-judicial lives, and that the prestige and authority of the office may not be used to enhance personal relationships, or for selfish reasons, or to bestow favors.[64] We are fortunate in this small state to have had relatively few instances of breaches in judicial ethics. On the other hand, it should never be forgotten how fragile our systems of laws and government are, and how much our system of governance relies on honest, ethical judges to fairly apply the law without bias or prejudice.

---

63   *In re Hill,* 152 Vt. 571 (1989)

64   Id.

# APPENDIX A:

Morse Opinion Disqualifying Wheel (December 27, 1984)

OF VERMONT

TTENDEN COUNTY, ss.

| | | |
|---|---|---|
| STATE OF VERMONT | ) | CHITTENDEN SUPERIOR COURT |
| | ) | |
| v. | ) | DOCKET NO. S1-83CnCr |
| | ) | |
| GORDON HUNT | ) | |

## OPINION AND ORDER

The Defendant has moved to disqualify the Assistant Judges in this case.

A hearing on the Motion was held on December 17, 1984. The State was represented by Terry Trono, Esq., Washington County State's Attorney, and Robert V. Simpson, Jr., Esq., Assistant Attorney General; the Defendant was represented by Robert Gaston, Esq.

At the hearing, the parties agreed that two depositions, one of John J. Easton, Vermont Attorney General, and the other of Charles Bristow, former Deputy Attorney General, be admitted as evidence and the same were filed with the Court. No other evidence was submitted.

# APPENDIX A *(continued)*

2.

## I. JURISDICTION

It is not improper for the Judge whose impartiality is challenged to determine, "on the basis of her own responsibility, the issue of her own recusal." Daitchman v. Daitchman, 144 Vt. ___ (1984). In this case, both Assistant Judges have declined to recuse themselves.

It then becomes the duty of the Presiding Judge to decide whether as a matter of law or mixed law and fact disqualification is required. Section 112(b) of Title 4, recently enacted (effective April 27, 1984), states in relevant part:

> In all proceedings, questions of law shall be decided by the presiding judge. In cases not tried before a jury, questions of fact shall be decided by the court. Mixed questions of law and fact shall be deemed to be questions of law. The presiding judge alone shall decide which are questions of law, questions of fact, and mixed questions of law and fact. (emphasis supplied)

In this Motion to Disqualify Assistant Judges, the facts have been determined without any fact-finding function by the Court. All the facts, as agreed by the parties, are contained in the record thus far, including two depositions. It is a question of law[1] what legal significance this evidence has, and in viewing this evidence the Court is to deem it true and make reasonable inferences from it in a light most favorable to the moving party.[2] Also, as agreed by the parties, even hearsay contained in the depositions may be considered, and, consequently, must be deemed to be true.

-346-

# APPENDIX A *(continued)*

3.

This is not to say that the facts deemed to be true in this opinion are in fact true. The purpose of a motion to disqualify a judge is different from proceedings to discipline a judge for unethical behavior. See Rules of Supreme Court for Disciplinary Control of Judges, 12 V.S.A. App. 1, Pt. IV. We are concerned here with the appearance of partiality and the right of a defendant in a criminal proceeding to be tried by a tribunal free of such appearance.

# APPENDIX A *(continued)*

4.

## II. THE FACTS

On August 11, 1983, the Chittenden Superior Court rejected a proffered plea-agreement between the State and the Defendant by a decision of two to one. The Presiding Judge's decision was to accept the plea agreement, while the Assistant Judges decided to reject it. There followed an interlocutory appeal to the Vermont Supreme Court wherein both parties challenged the authority of the Assistant Judges to reject the agreement. Order dated August 30, 1983. The decision of the high Court was filed on May 11, 1984, upholding the power of the Assistant Judges to reject the agreement. State v. Hunt, 144 Vt. ___ (1984). The mandate was stayed until November 2, 1984, during the pendency of a petition for a writ of certiorari to the United States Supreme Court, which petition was denied on October 1, 1984.

The merits of the appeal to the Vermont Supreme Court were briefed by the parties and two entities acting as "friends of the court" arguing against the exercise of power by the Assistant Judges, namely, the Defendant (Brief dated October 26, 1983); the State (Brief dated December 8, 1983); the Vermont Bar Association, as amicus curiae (Brief filed December 13, 1983); and the Vermont Chapter of the American Civil Liberties Union, as amicus curiae (Brief dated October 21, 1983). The only brief submitted to the appellate court arguing in favor of the exercise of Assistant-Judge power was that of the Vermont Association of Assistant Judges (Brief dated December 2, 1983).

# APPENDIX A *(continued)*

5.

The Assistant Judges Association had retained F. Ray Keyser, Jr., Esq., to represent its interest in State v. Hunt in the Vermont Supreme Court, and its amicus brief was prepared by Joseph A. Dickinson, Esq., in association with Mr. Keyser.

Sometime during the Fall (late October or November) of 1983, Assistant Judge Jane L. Wheel, who at that time was both a sitting Judge on the Hunt case and the President of the Assistant Judges Association, called the Attorney General, John Easton, to arrange for a meeting with him to discuss the Assistant Judges' brief. Within a week the meeting was held. Easton Transcript at 2-3.

At that meeting, which lasted about a half hour or less and included only Mr. Easton and Judge Wheel, Judge Wheel requested that the Attorney General join in the brief of the Assistant Judges Association and explained the merits of its position. Id. at 7-8.

Attorney General Easton responded by saying he did not want to participate with the Association because he did not want to "appear [to] undermine the role of the prosecutor." Id. at 9.

Judge Wheel continued at that meeting to attempt to persuade Mr. Easton to defend the Assistant Judges' position and, as Mr. Easton recalls, said in effect:

> She described the size of their organization
> of Assistant Judges and how all of the Assistant
> Judges felt very strongly about this principle
> and all these people could be very helpful to
> me, that she herself would like to help me in my
> political end.

Id. at 16-17.

# APPENDIX A *(continued)*

6.

Thereafter, in a telephone conversation with Mr. Keyser, the lawyer for the Assistant Judges Association, Attorney Keyser mentioned "that his clients exercise a fair amount of political influence in their particular...counties." Id. at 18. At that point, Mr. Easton told Mr. Keyser he would "give a fresh look at the situation" and requested a copy of the brief to review. Id.

After the Association's brief was reviewed by Charles Bristow, the Attorney General's Deputy, Mr. Easton decided, after consultation with Mr. Bristow, to not join in the brief. Id. at 19.

Sometime after this decision was communicated by Mr. Bristow to Mr. Keyser, Judge Wheel and Mr. Bristow had a telephone conversation wherein the Judge was told of the Attorney General's decision and Judge Wheel said, according to Mr. Bristow:

> She did say something to the effect that the
> Assistant Judges' Association felt strongly
> about this issue and that it would be clear as
> to those who were supporters of their position
> and as to those who were not, and that if John
> Easton didn't join there might be possible
> political ramifications for him.

Bristow Tr. at 8.

The oral argument to the Vermont Supreme Court occurred on December 14, 1983.

A letter dated December 15, 1983, from Charles Bristow on behalf of the Attorney General to the Chief Justice was sent. It stated:

# APPENDIX A *(continued)*

7.

After reviewing the briefs filed in connection
with this case, wh' h number four in favor of
disqualification . assistant judges at the plea
bargaining phase of a criminal proceeding and
one opposed to the assistant judges' disqualification, the Office of the Attorney General wishes
to communicate its availability as an _amicus_ _curiae_
on behalf of the assistant judges.

While the Office recognizes that the Court was
provided with briefs on both sides of the issue
and also had the benefit of oral argument from
the parties, the Office of the Attorney General,
nevertheless, wishes to make itself available as
a resource charged with the defense of the Vermont
Constitution and its officers. In that capacity,
should the Court seek further briefing on behalf
of the assistant judges, the Office would accept
such an invitation.

Mr. Bristow received a short letter reply from the Chief

Justice "to the effect that the Attorney General's office is free

to do whatever it wants." _Id._ at 10.

During a conversation with the Chief Justice about "the

letters," Mr. Bristow was told

that Judge Wheel had contacted him about the case
and that his response was it was totally inappropriate for her to do so and he wouldn't discuss
it with her.

_Id._ at 16. 3/

# APPENDIX A *(continued)*

8.

III. THE LAW AND THE CODE OF JUDICIAL
CONDUCT (12 V.S.A. App. VIII, A.O. 10)

The gravamen of Defendant's Motion to Disqualify is the direction of Canon 3C(1) of the Code of Judicial Conduct that

> [a] judge should disqualify himself in a proceeding in which his impartiality might reasonably be questioned....

Former Chief Justice Barney in reflecting upon Canon 3C wrote:

> Disqualification is a sensitive concern for judges, and if the slightest question exists, all doubts should be resolved in its favor.

Condosta v. Condosta, 137 Vt. 35, 36 (1979).

The single most important ingredient which gives the judiciary its legitimate place as a separate and independent branch of government is impartiality. More than common sense, wisdom, and intelligence, we want our judges to be as impartial as is practically feasible.

This is reflected in Section 28 of the Vermont Constitution:

> The Courts of Justice shall be open for the trial of all causes proper for their cognizance; and justice shall be therein impartially administered, without corruption, or unnecessary delay.

As stated in Leonard v. Willcox, 101 Vt. 195, 213 (1928), quoting from an earlier case,

> "Every man is entitled by law not only to a fair trial of his case, but to one as free as may be from suspicion of partiality."

> Section 28 of our Constitution, quoted above, is declaratory of this principle.

# APPENDIX A *(continued)*

9.

Impartiality is the objective balance of view toward persons and issues uncluttered with biases for or prejudices against them. This does not mean, however, that judges must be perfectly impartial because, as human beings, judges cannot help being somewhat susceptible to influences which affect their balance of view. But, it is incumbent upon a judge to step aside when the circumstances are such that it would be reasonable for an objective observer to conclude that the judge's decision-making ability might be suspect. That is the admonition of Canon 3C.

The best statement of the standard to be applied is found in United States v. Cowden, 545 F.2d 257, 265 (1st Cir. 1976), discussing the federal rule governing the disqualification of a judge, which is in all material respects identical to Canon 3C.

> The proper test...is whether the charge of lack of impartiality is grounded on facts that would create a reasonable doubt concerning the judge's impartiality, not in the mind of the judge himself or even necessarily in the mind of the litigant filing the motion... but rather in the mind of the reasonable [person].

The issue here centers on preserving the integrity of a criminal case to ensure as best as is feasible that the accused and the State receive fair-objective treatment by the judiciary.

The State argues that Judge Wheel's conduct did not amount to a "personal bias or prejudice concerning a party," and that her conduct resulted solely from her position on the judicial power of Assistant Judges. Canon 3C(1)(a).

# APPENDIX A *(continued)*

10.

The State, however, misses a point; "personal bias or
prejudice" for or against a party is not the only reason requiring disqualification on the ground of partiality. [4/]

Canon 1 states:

> An independent and honorable judiciary is
> indispensable to justice in our society. A
> judge should participate in establishing,
> maintaining, and enforcing, and should himself
> observe, high standards of conduct so that the
> integrity and independence of the judiciary may
> be preserved. The provisions of this Code should
> be construed and applied to further that objective.

Canon 2 states in part:

> A judge should respect and comply with the
> law and should conduct himself at all times in
> a manner that promotes public confidence in the
> integrity and impartiality of the judiciary.

Canon 3A states in part:

> (1) A judge. . .should be unswayed by partisan
> interests.

> (4) A judge should accord to every person who
> is legally interested in a proceeding, or his
> lawyer, full right to be heard according to law,
> and, except as authorized by law, neither initiate
> nor consider ex parte or other communications
> concerning a pending or impending proceeding.

Viewing the evidence in this matter as true for purposes
of the motion, there is no doubt that violations of Canons 1, 2
and 3 are established.

Ex parte communications to influence the outcome of a case
by one judge to another is unethical. See The Florida Bar v.
McCain, 361 So.2d 700 (1978)(Undermines judicial process and

-34-

# APPENDIX A *(continued)*

11.

erodes public confidence in the integrity and impartiality of
the judiciary) (Canons 1, 2A and 3A(4)); see also Dixon v. State
Commission on Judicial Conduct, 47 N.Y.2d 523, 393 N.E.2d 441
(1979).

While the record does not establish what was said to the
Chief Justice by Judge Wheel, the contact was about the Hunt
appeal and the Chief Justice's reaction leads to a reasonable
inference that the conduct was intended to influence the course
of the proceedings.

A judge who employs threats of political influence to
persuade a public official to take particular action violates
these standards. See Shilling v. State Commission on Judicial
Conduct, 51 N.Y.2d 397, 415 N.E.2d 900, 902 (1980), wherein it
is written:

> "[a]ny conduct, on or off the Bench, inconsistent
> with proper judicial demeanor subjects the judi-
> ciary as a whole to disrespect and impairs the
> usefulness of the individual Judge to carry out
> his or her constitutionally mandated function"...

It is only the Defendant who at this point complains
about the conduct of Judge Wheel, but, this is not to say that
the prosecution should be voicing satisfaction with the status
quo of the Court.

It is evident why a trial of the Defendant here is darkly
clouded by the participation of Judge Wheel.

The plea agreement was a compromise which became a goal for
both parties to resolve the question of guilt and the sentence
to be imposed.

-355-

# APPENDIX A *(continued)*

12.

When the parties appealed the Assistant Judges' decision to reject that agreement, both the defense and the prosecution had hope that the decision would be reversed during the normal course of the appellate process.

Neither party expected that the appellate process would be jeopardized by political influences in the form and substance of ex parte communications by one of the trial judges sitting in the case.

It is insufficient to say that Judge Wheel's behavior probably did not influence the result of the Hunt appeal. There is the possibility that it did and at least there is the appearance of impropriety, because the conduct was directed toward influencing the result of the appeal.

Is it fair to the Defendant or the State for Judge Wheel to make further rulings in this litigation. I think not. She has not recused herself from sitting and, consequently, what assurance do the parties have that she will not try to influence future rulings in the case as she did in the past appeal?

The conclusion that Judge Wheel should be disqualified is buttressed by the fact that at the hearing on the question of her disqualification, Judge Wheel made allegations that the Attorney General, who is representing the State, violated her lawyer-client privilege and that Robert Gaston, who is representing the Defendant, should be disqualified because he has a conflict of interest.

# APPENDIX A *(continued)*

12.

When the parties appealed the Assistant Judges' decision to reject that agreement, both the defense and the prosecution had hope that the decision would be reversed during the normal course of the appellate process.

Neither party expected that the appellate process would be jeopardized by political influences in the form and substance of ex parte communications by one of the trial judges sitting in the case.

It is insufficient to say that Judge Wheel's behavior probably did not influence the result of the Hunt appeal. There is the possibility that it did and at least there is the appearance of impropriety, because the conduct was directed toward influencing the result of the appeal.

Is it fair to the Defendant or the State for Judge Wheel to make further rulings in this litigation. I think not. She has not recused herself from sitting and, consequently, what assurance do the parties have that she will not try to influence future rulings in the case as she did in the past appeal?

The conclusion that Judge Wheel should be disqualified is buttressed by the fact that at the hearing on the question of her disqualification, Judge Wheel made allegations that the Attorney General, who is representing the State, violated her lawyer-client privilege and that Robert Gaston, who is representing the Defendant, should be disqualified because he has a conflict of interest.

# APPENDIX A *(continued)*

13.

These allegations were not made to defend her conduct in
any way and the timing of them tends to show a lack of impartiality toward both parties in the case.

Simply put, what happened here was political rather than
judicial. While a judge may in confined and circumspect ways
act in a political sense from time to time, see. e.g., Canon 4,
he or she must maintain scrupulous neutrality about issues in a
case in which he or she sits. Once a judge allows political
action to contaminate his or her judicial function over an issue
in a case, the judge's neutrality is objectively in question;
when this happens the appearance of an impartial tribunal is in
doubt and the judge should take no further part in the proceedings.

# APPENDIX A *(continued)*

14.

The record does not support a conclusion that Assistant Judge Charles L. Delaney should be disqualified. The only connection with Judge Wheel's conduct is that he was a member of the Assistant Judges Association of which Judge Wheel was President at the time.

It is ADJUDGED AND ORDERED as follows:

The Motion to Disqualify Assistant Judges is GRANTED as to Judge Jane L. Wheel and DENIED as to Judge Charles L. Delaney.

Dated: December 27, 1984.

James L. Morse,
Superior Court Judge

# APPENDIX B:
## Amestoy Letter to Chief Justice Allen (November 30, 1985)

*JEFFREY L. AMESTOY*
*ATTORNEY GENERAL*
**BRIAN L. BURGESS**
*oluun ATTORNEY GENERAL*
*WIULIAMLGKIffIN*

*CHIEF ASS?. ATTORNEY GENERAL*

*ꝑ. Hayes*

**STATE OF** *VERMONT*
*OFFICE OF THE ATTORNEY GENERAL*
*110 STATE STREET*
*MONTPELIER*
*05402*
*TEL.: m2420-3171*

November 20, 1985

PERSONAL AND CONFIDENTIAL

Honorable Frederic W. Allen
Chief Justice.
Vermont Supreme Court
111 State Street
Montpelier, Vermont 05602

Dear Chief Justice Allen:

   I am writing to inform you that the Attorney General's Office has received allegations of possible improper conduct on the part of a member of the Vermont Judiciary, Chittenden Circuit, Assistant Judge Jane Wheel. The allegations received also involve potential criminal conduct. None of the allegations have yet been substantiated, however the Attorney General's Office will be continuing to look into the matter.

JLA/DTS/mb

Since 1 your s,

JEF    . AMESTOY
A o ne General

# APPENDIX C:
## Hill Memorandum to Other Justices (December 30, 1985)

MEMORANDUM

TO:    Frederic W. Allen, Chief Justice
       Louis P. Peck, Associate Justice
       Ernest W. Gibson III, Associate Justice
       Thomas L. Hayes, Associate Justice

FROM: William C. Hill, Associate Justice

DATE: December 30, 1985

_____

Justices Hill, Gibson, and Hayes having been designated as a committeDto define the term "official duties" to guide the presiding judges in verifying the accounts of the assistant judges, suggest that the definition of "official duties", as used in 32 V.S.A. § 1141, should be as follows:

> Attendance at a superior court when necessary to
>
> the advancement of the disposition of any action
>
> between litigants or at any function desirable or
>
> necessary to the operation or betterment of the
>
> Judicial Branch.

### GUIDELINES

We find that language cannot be precise enough to specify all the possible circumstances wherein assistant judges will have earned state compensation for having performed official duties. Sane discretion therefore must be placed in the presiding judge.

Without limitation, the following are not to be considered official duties

for purposes of state compensation:

# APPENDIX C *(continued)*

Signing notarial certificates; county administra-

tive duties, such as purchasing supplies or equip-

ment or hiring personnel, which duties should be

paid for by the county.

Without limitation, examples of the following duties could be considered as official:

Attendance at a judicial committee meeting; attend-

ance at a legislative meeting; [attendance at

*Itt-L p*

oourtIduring the normal work week even though a

superior judge is not present; attendance at court

during the normal work week for a scheduled judi-

cial proceeding even though the proceeding is sub-

sequently cancelled; attendance at court during

other times when present for duty with a superior

judge.

# APPENDIX D:
## Supreme Court Memorandum to Superior Court Judges
## (February 3, 1986)

SUPREME COURT OF VERMONT                (802) 828–3276

Mailing Address:
111 State Street
c/o State Office Bldg. P. O.
Montpelier, VT 05602

### MEMORANDUM

TO:        Superior Judges

FROM:      Supreme Court

RE:        Definition of 'Official Duties'

DATE:      February 3, 1986

For the purposes of 4 V.S.A. S 655, 'Official Duties' as used in 32 V.S.A. S 1141 are defined as follows:

> Attendance at a superior court when necessary to the advancement of the disposition of any action between litigants or at any function desirable or necessary to the operation or betterment of the Judicial Branch.

We find that language cannot be precise enough to specify all the possible circumstances wherein assistant judges rill have earned state compensation for having performed official duties. Some discretion therefore must be placed in the presiding judge. The presiding judge, however, may accept representations of any person whose account he must approve.

# APPENDIX E:
## Chief Justice Allen Letter to Thomas P. Salmon

**SUPREME COURT OF VERMONT**
**111 STATE STREET**
**MONTPELIER, VERMONT**
**05602**

☐ Pltf. ☐ Deft. ☒ ~~Status~~
Exhibit No. 8 ___ For I. D.
A. M. ~~DeSerres~~ N. P. *FeeTevc*
Witness *Justice Allen*
Date *9/9/86*

CHAMBERS OF
**FREDERIC W. ALLEN**
CHIEF JUSTICE

February 10, 1986

Hon. Thomas P. Salmon
Chairman
Judicial Conduct Board
P.O. Box 535
Bellows Falls, VT 05101

Dear Mr. Salmon:

You are hereby requested to investigate allegations in the media that an assistant judge in Chittenden Superior Court has collected fees pursuant to 32 V.S.A. § 1141 for days when she did not attend court or engage in the performance of her official duties. These allegations constitute a complaint charging a violation of one or more of the acts of misconduct set forth in Rule 2 of this Court's Order effective November 3, 1981.

I would request that the investigation extend over the entire year of 1985, and that it determine whether the assistant judges in that court have collected fees to which they were not entitled.

It has been brought to my attention that there may have been difficulties with the recordkeeping and/or computer operation which may possibly have led to inaccuracies concerning the number of days actually spent by those judges in the performance of their duties. I am enclosing a copy of a letter from Judge Wheel addressing these concerns. As it may be a somewhat difficult task for an investigator to understand and comprehend a court docket and the various entries therein, I am prepared to offer whatever assistance from within the judicial branch as may be necessary to assist in your work.

I would further anticipate that the resolution of the ultimate question of whether or not there has been misconduct may depend, in part, on the meaning of "official duties" as set forth in 32 V.S.A. § 114(a). The Court is prepared to offer its definition of these words should that become necessary.

Very truly yours,

Frederic W. Allen
Chief Justice

FWA:ab

# APPENDIX F:
## Supreme Court Letter to Amestoy

SUPREME COURT OF VERMONT
III STATE STREET
1ER VERMONT
00102

CHAMBERS OF
FREDERIC W. ALLEN
CHIEF JUSTICE

May 28, 1986

Jeffrey L. Amestoy
Attorney General
Pavilion Office Building
Montpelier, Vermont 05602

Dear Mr. Attorney General:

I wish to express the deep concern of the Court over the length of time that has passed since an investigation was announced concerning the activities of an Assistant Judge of the Chittenden Superior Court. Because suggestions of improper conduct upon the part of a judicial officer tend to cast a cloud upon the entire Judiciary, we would request and urge that this matter be resolved at the earliest possible date consistent with the obligations imposed upon your office, and that the necessary time and resources be utilized to accomplish this. We assume that you have been afforded all necessary cooperation from the Judicial Branch during the course of your investigation, and assure you of our cooperation in this regard in the future.

We are further concerned about the disclosures appearing in the media pertaining to an inquest in this matter. As this Court has indicated in the past, it is the policy of the law that secrecy is mandated in these proceedings. We assume that you have taken, or will take, appropriate steps to insure that such disclosures cannot be attributed to your office.

We trust that this letter will be received in the spirit in which it is intended. We do not mean to suggest how you should perform your duties. We do, however, wish to make clear our belief that it is of utmost importance to the integrity of the judicial system that this matter be brought to a conclusion as soon as this can be reasonably accomplished.

WCH:ab

Very truly yours,

For the Chief Justice
William C. Hill, Associate Justice

# APPENDIX G:

## Moran Affidavit (June 19, 1986)

21.1-1-REV L. AMESTOY
*4110110'4 fl ©11141*

BRIAN L. BURGESS
Pt rilt *4111INMI GIVIRAL*

WILUAME.GRIFFIN
*CHILI ABST. ATTONHUA GINER4I*

STATE OF VERMONT
OFFICE OF THE ATTORNEY GENERAL
109 STATE STREET
MONTPELIER
05602
TEL.: 802-020-3171

June 18, 1986

Mary Kennedy, Clerk
Vermont District Court, Orange Circuit
Orange County Courthouse
Chelsea, Vermont 05038

Re: Inquest Proceedings: In re Chittenden County Superior Court

Dear Mary:

Enclosed for filing are the application for Nontestimonial Identification Order and Supporting Affidavits presented to Judge Levitt and the Nontestimonial Identification Order signed by Judge Levitt concerning the above-noted abo ve- no ted matt. . 4 , 1

Since these materialqare part an inquest proceeding and contain inquest matters, .hey should be sealed within the inquest and kept secret pursuant to statute.

S ncerely yours,

PHILLIP J. 04'KO
Assistant Attorney General

PJC/rmd

Enc.

SO ORDERED:

Judge' Linda Levitt

# APPENDIX G *(continued)*

AFFIDAVIT

Randall R. Moran, affiant states that I am a certified law enforcement officer and a full time State Investigator with the Vermont Attorney General's Office. I have held this position since January 1979. Prior to that I was employed by the Burlington Police Department, from 1970 to 1979.

In November of 1985, this affiant was assigned to investigate allegations that Assistant Judge Jane Wheel of Chittenden County, State of Vermont, had charged the State of Vermont for per diem on days that she did not work. This affiant interviewed several people in this investigation, and one of them was Francis Fee, the Clerk of Chittenden Superior Court.

Mr. Fee produced for this affiant, copies of Judge Jane Wheels' expense accounts and, by going into the computer system at the Chittenden Superior Court, Mr. Fee produced for this affiant the number of cases that Judge Jane Wheel alledgedly sat on from January 1985 through June 1985. The statistics were broken down by the month and this showed each case that Judge Wheel sat on and what day.

Mr. Fee explained the jacket file system at Chittenden Superior Court as the following. What ever happens on a

# APPENDIX G *(continued)*

particular case is noted on the front of the file jacket by
a scheduling clerk.The date is entered first, then what
took place and then who was present. The Superior Court
Judge is listed, then the Assistant Judge, if one was
present, and the Court Reporter, if there was one, and then
the scheduling clerks initials.

Assistant Attorney General David Tartter and this
affiant went into Chittenden Superior Court and reviewed
all the files that were on the docket sheets from 3-5-85
through 4-12-85. The statistics presented to us by Francis
Fee had shown, during this period of time, that Judge Wheel
did not sit on one case. In our review of the jacket
files, we found no record that Judge Wheel sat on any case
during the above time period, and no record that she signed
any orders.

On January 15, 1986, Francis Fee showed this writer a
file jacket, S326-85 Cnd, where Judge Wheels' name was
added to an entry'on 10-30-85. Mr. Fee stated that he
recognizes the signature as Judge Wheels'. Judge Katz name
was added also, apparently by the same person who wrote
Judge Wheels' name. According to Mr. Fee, Judge Katz was
shown the entry, and he crossed out Judge Wheels' name
along with his own and wrote on the jacket file: "entered

# APPENDIX G *(continued)*

incorrectly on 1-9-86. Crossed out 1-10-86 per M Katz".

There were three other jacket files found with Judge Wheels' name apparently added inappropriately when the record shows that she did not attend the hearing. Each signature on the jacket file appears to be the signature of Judge Jane Wheel. Also found were two orders inside the jacket file, apparently signed by Judge Wheel when, again according to the system, she did not attend the hearing. One of the orders, in case S1159-84 Cnc, was apparently signed by Judge Wheel, and this affiant retrieved copies of the original orders issued at the proceeding to both of the lawyers involved, and these copies do not have Judge Wheels' signature on it. The Presiding Judge was David Jenkins, and a interview with him, he stated that if an Assistant Judge is not present at a hearing, he puts a squiggle mark under his signature. The order that Judge Wheel allegedly signed in the file, clearly shows that she signed the order through the squiggle mark. The order was dated 3-6-85, which is in the time period that we are looking at.

The entries that were added with Judge Wheels' name appeared to have been made after the initial entry by the scheduling clerk. The writing is different from the

# APPENDIX G *(continued)*

clerk's and the instrument used to write the entry is
different also.

In interviewing a number Superior Court Judges and a
number Assistant Judges throughout the State of Vermont,
this affiant was told that the name of a Judge should only
appear on the jacket file if he or she attended the hearing
for which the entry is made. The only way an Assistant
Judge should sign an order is if he or she attended the
proceeding out of which the order arose.

On 2-25-86, Lee Suskin of the Court Administators
Office was interviewed at the Attorney General's Office.
Mr. Suskin was appointed by the Supreme Court to conduct a
study of the Chittenden Superior Court concerning some
problems and complaints that have been recieved over the

past few months. Mr. Suskin stated that he has interviewed
several people in Chittenden Superior Court, including
Judge Jane Wheel. Mr. Suskin stated that Judge Wheel spoke
of the jacket entries and how messed up they are and the
fact that she and her husband has had to go in on weekends
and correct some of the jacket entries on the files.

On 5-28-86, This affiant interviewed Judge Mathew Katz,
a Superior Court Judge and he stated that he was present
and watched Judge Jane Wheel inappropriately add her name

# APPENDIX G *(continued)*

and his to a file jacket at a time subsequent to the date
of the entry to which the names were added. Judge Katz
stated further that the day after, he crossed the names out
and wrote in that the entry was put in incorrectly and
signed his name. This affiant showed Judge Katz a copy of
the file jacket cover and he identified it as the one that
Judge Wheel added her name to.

## C4tRit ____
Affiant
19 \99G·

Subscribed and sworn to before me this _____ day of

June, 1986.

_____
Judicial Officer

# APPENDIX H:

## Hayes Letter to Lerner (June 24, 1986)

SUPREME COURT OF VERMONT
111 STATE STREET
MONTPELIER, VERMONT
05602

CHAMBERS OF
THOMAS L. HAYES
ASSOCIATE JUSTICE

MEMORANDUM

TO:     Thomas J. Lehner, Court Administrator

FROM:   Thomas L. Hayes, Associate Justice

DATE:   June 24, 1986

     I have just learned that a false swearing investigation directed at Judge Wheel is under way based in large part on an affidavit of Randy Moran who claims that Lee Suskin contends that he was told that he, Suskin, was told by Judge Wheel that she altered the jacket entries on certain case files. As I understand it, only Lee Suskin has made any claim to the effect that Judge Wheel made a statement of this kind.

     Do you know anything about this situation and, if so, what do you know about it and when did you find out about it?

TLH:lfa

www.ingramcontent.com/pod-product-compliance
Lightning Source LLC
Chambersburg PA
CBHW060307220326
41598CB00027B/4259